Road to Redemption
The Key Is Christ

Scriptures are quoted from the following translations:
Modern King James Version (MKJV), Literal Translation Version (LITV), New International Version (NIV), New Living Translation (NLT), Bible in Basic English (BBE), International Standard Version (ISV), King James Version (KJV), American Standard Version (ASV), Contemporary English Version (CEV), English Standard Version (ESV)

©2009 Beautiful Fields Publications
All Rights Reserved.

This book may not be copied or reprinted for commercial gain or profit.

Cover image ©2008 Andrew Bergen, used with permission.

Contents

Dedication	4
My Prayer For You	5
Disclaimer	6
Psalm 139	7
IN THE BEGINNING WAS CHRIST	8
Daddy No	12
Knocking At Death's Door	23
The Dream	29
Enough Is Enough	31
Cross Roads-On The Brink Of No Return	38
Beginning Of The End	49
I Have Loved You Since The Day I Conceived You	53
False Identity	63
Temptations Of Babylon	72
The Dream Fulfilled	82
I Do	93
The Walls Begin To Crumble	96
On The Edge	108
Hope Restored-Faith Renewed	112
Return To Righteousness	121
Standing On The Word	132
Love Covers	138
FREEDOM IN CHRIST	152

Dedication

This book first and foremost dedicated to Jesus Christ who saved me, to my husband for his ongoing support, to my family who I treasure and to my friends who were with me along the way. May those who read through my journey find Jehovah {who}is my strength, my fortress, my deliverer; my God, my rock; {who}I will trust in; {who} is my shield, the horn of my salvation, and my high tower. Psalm 18:2

My Prayer for You

Jesus, I pray for anyone one who reads this book who does not know that they are in spiritual bondage, just as I did not know, Jesus I pray you will take the blinders off of their eyes too so they may receive their freedom which is in you and you alone. Thank you, Jesus, for your sacrifice you made on the cross, for my freedom and theirs. I thank you, for loving us enough to set us free, so we may come to know and love you. I cannot thank you enough for this precious person who is reading my testimony, may they know that there is nothing under heaven that they have done or ever will do that will ever separate Your love from them. I ask that the Holy Spirit will teach you and minister to you while you read through my journey on this road to redemption. Jesus I pray blessings over this precious person, in Your Name. Amen

Disclaimer

This testimony is written to the best of my memory in chronological order. I do believe the Holy Spirit continually led me while writing this testimony. Most of the names of people and cities have been changed to protect the identity of my church & nuclear families as well as friends who have been profoundly affected by the contents of my testimony. My desire is not to harm or dishonor any of my parents including my biological father, mother or adoptive father, pastors or the church. The scriptures say we are to cover our parents rather than expose them (Genesis 9:20-27). I pray the Lord covers everyone who has played a role in my life resulting in a testimony which I believe has the potential to heal many people who have lived with sexual perversion and substance abuse. I pray if you do not know Jesus or believe you have done too much to be forgiven, you will come to understand Jesus died for all of your sins and all are forgiven through the love of Jesus Christ. I pray the Holy Spirit will cover you while you read through the book and Father God will draw you closer to Himself. I ask these things in the name of His only begotten son, Jesus Christ.

Psalm 139 NIV

You have searched me, LORD, and you know me. You know when I sit and when I rise; you perceive my thoughts from afar. You discern my going out and my lying down; you are familiar with all my ways. Before a word is on my tongue you, LORD, know it completely. You hem me in behind and before, and you lay your hand upon me. Such knowledge is too wonderful for me, too lofty for me to attain. Where can I go from your Spirit? Where can I flee from your presence? If I go up to the heavens, you are there; if I make my bed in the depths, you are there. If I rise on the wings of the dawn, if I settle on the far side of the sea, even there your hand will guide me, your right hand will hold me fast. If I say, "Surely the darkness will hide me and the light become night around me," even the darkness will not be dark to you; the night will shine like the day, for darkness is as light to you. For you created my inmost being; you knit me together in my mother's womb. I praise you because I am fearfully and wonderfully made; your works are wonderful, I know that full well. My frame was not hidden from you when I was made in the secret place, when I was woven together in the depths of the earth. Your eyes saw my unformed body; all the days ordained for me were written in your book before one of them came to be. How precious to me are your thoughts, God! How vast is the sum of them! Were I to count them, they would outnumber the grains of sand— when I awake, I am still with you. If only you, God, would slay the wicked! Away from me, you who are bloodthirsty! They speak of you with evil intent; your adversaries misuse your name. Do I not hate those who hate you, LORD, and abhor those who are in rebellion against you? I have nothing but hatred for them; I count them my enemies. Search me, God, and know my heart; test me and know my anxious thoughts. See if there is any offensive way in me, and lead me in the way everlasting.

In The Beginning Was Christ

In the beginning was the Word, and the Word was with God, and the Word was God. John 1:1 MJKV

Jesus was always with me as a child. I loved talking and spending countless hours with Him. I was so in love with Jesus, the One who knew me from the beginning of time. Often I would take my little tape recorder, place my favorite gospel tape in the player and tuck it under my pillow. How blessed I felt to just worship God in the safety of my little room. The sounds of heaven would circle through my bedroom and I knew Jesus was there. The peace that enveloped me was so surreal. Every inch of my body was wrapped in His love. I knew He was greater than the universe which lies in the dark, wilder than the passions in human hearts, and I was just a tiny spark. This spark would blaze through the universe just to join the One who made me.

Often I would visit Jesus in heaven. He would hold my hand and walk me through the gardens. They were beautiful. The flowers were plentiful and not a single weed in sight. We would laugh and play together. I remember how strong and beautiful Jesus seemed to me; full of life and joy. How happy He was just to be with me. I would gather bouquets of flowers, as we walked along hand in hand, carefully selecting each flower I would give to Jesus.

I remember one time being very frustrated with Jesus and how patient He was with me. I desperately wanted Him to turn my dolls into babies. Knowing He could do it no problem, I could not figure out why He said no. At three or four years of age, I thought I could easily take care of a bunch of babies. Besides, I really loved babies and I took really good care of my dolls, I fed them, changed their diapers and their clothes. I thought I would make a really good mom. Eventually I got over the fact He did not want to make my dolls into babies and now many years later, I am very grateful He said no!

Days would pass by and I would tell my friends all about Jesus. How wonderful He is and how all they had to do was believe in Him, trust Him, say sorry for the bad things they did. I would tell them if they accepted Him as their savior then they too could be with Jesus forever.

There was one girl in particular who really wanted Jesus in her life. She lived just down the street from me and would often come over and play. I could not understand how she did not know Jesus. As we would color I would talk to her about Him. One day, as we were playing in my room she decided she too wanted to know Jesus. She wanted Him in her life forever! The sun was bright that day. As we knelt down in front of my bedroom window, leaning over the bed with hands clasped tightly, we prayed together. The sun shone on her in all its glory. As she prayed, heaven rejoiced and the angels danced. She asked Jesus to forgive her for her sins and to come into her life, so she too could love him forever. What an amazing experience; I would have another friend in heaven with me!

My relationship with Jesus continued to grow. Adults began to find out about my relationship with Christ and would often ask me questions about Him. Then one day God told me something I did not really understand. He told me to get baptized. I spoke with the elders in my church who were not immediately convinced a 6 year old should be baptized. One of the elders came to my house and sat with me at my dining room table. He seemed quite old to me. He asked my why I wanted to get baptized and I told him quite frankly God told me to get baptized. It was not very long after this conversation I was water baptized.

Jesus, soon after, appeared before me in the middle of the night. He always knew where to find me- even if I was sleeping in front of the blow heater in the living room! He stood in the middle of the living room dressed in white, with a blue sash beautifully adorned across His shoulder. Jesus' arms were stretched out towards me, but I could not reach Him. As I tried to go to Him the brown leather pillows from the couch began to swirl in between us. There seemed to be no way of getting to my beloved Jesus and I was completely grieved; as was He.

After that night, my Christ centered life changed, and things were never the same again…

In all things God works for the good of those who love Him, who have been called according to His purpose.
~Romans 8:28~

Daddy, No!

This is why our fathers have fallen by the sword and why our sons and daughters and our wives are in captivity.
2 Chronicles 29:9

Every child I know loves the story of "The Three Little Pigs" except for me...

Late one night my dad came into my room to tell me the story of the three little pigs. *Once upon a time there lived the three little pigs...*my dad said in his deep voice. *They went to live in the forest. The first pig built his house out of straw. The second little pig made his house out of sticks and the third little pig made his house out of bricks. One day along came a big bad WOLF! He knocked on the door of the first little pig. "Little Pig, Little Pig, let me in." "Not by the hair of my chinny, chin, chin!" "Then I'll Huff and I'll Puff and I'll blow your house in!"* At this point my dad lifted up my nightgown and blew on my tummy. I started laughing as his whiskers tickled my stomach. *The little pig ran as fast as he could to his brother's house. Then along came the Big Bad WOLF! Knock, Knock, Knock! "Little pigs, you let me in!" "Not by the hairs of our chinny, chin, chins!" "Then I'll huff and I'll puff and I'll blow your house in!"* My dad then blew on my tummy again. Again I giggled as the vibrations tickled my stomach. *The little pigs ran as quickly as they could to their brother's house. Then along came the Big Bad WOLF! He banged on the door. "Little Pigs, little pigs, let me come in! And the little pigs said, "Not by the hair of our chinny, chin, chins!" "Then I'll huff and I'll puff and I'll blow your house in!"*

I charge you: Do not arouse or awaken love till it is ready. Solomon's Song of Songs 8:4

At this point my dad started blowing on my stomach. He pulled down my covers a little further (I did not wear underwear that night when I went to bed). My dad then blew on parts he never should have seen. My memory begins to fade after that.

My body felt different than it used to after that night. I was aware of my private parts now and often played with them. It felt weird, and good, and bad all at the same time. My mom would sometimes catch me and scold me for it. I couldn't figure out why she was mad at me. One day I was playing with little dolls and I got the idea in my head of putting my dolls face on my private parts. I didn't know why I was doing this, I didn't really want to, but I did it all the same. I didn't know who I was anymore.

Life became increasingly more difficult and I could no longer find Jesus. It was as if someone had not only taken my friend away from me, but slowly also began to take my memory of Him as well.

My dad began to hug me in ways which made me feel very uncomfortable. The smell of his breath was vile, reeking with beer. As he would hug me, he would slowly let go and rub his hands over my chest. I felt more and more isolated. I never wanted to be alone with him, but I could not tell anyone either. The years continued on as did the sexual abuse. I was only a shadow of who I used to be when I would spend countless hours with Christ.

Now instead of inviting my friends over to talk about Jesus I would try and freak them out. I would have them convinced there was a whole other world I could tap into and if they didn't do as I said I would send creatures after them. I would say I could go in and out of this vortex that was in my wall. Then I would pretend to put my arm through the wall and somehow convinced my friends my arm was actually going through the wall. Sin had become my constant companion.

One afternoon I went to my friend Stan's who lived just around the corner from me. Our older siblings were also friends. His sister was babysitting him this particular afternoon. We were playing with his GI Joes, when his sister called me into the bathroom. I really like to be around older girls because I didn't have any sisters. So when an older girl paid attention to me it was the be-all-to-end-all.

I went into the bathroom and she closed the door behind us. She then turned and locked the door. I instinctively wanted out of the bathroom really badly. I asked her if I could leave the bathroom now and she said no. She took off her pants and her underwear commanding me to touch her. As I approached her naked body I remember her unzipping my pants and then the memory fades into nothingness.

Around grade three we moved into a four-plex that my parents converted into a massive house. We needed a large house to fit my five brothers, our foster kids, my parents and myself. Because of the chaos from the move, the abuse stopped for a short while. I am not sure exactly when the abuse started again, but I do remember an incident which may have triggered it. One day my dad told me he was going to give me a bath. I remember asking if mom could bathe me instead, but my dad was adamant he was going to bathe me. I remember my dad closing the door to the cold white bathroom and fear setting in. As he washed every inch of my body, I was violated all over again. All hope was lost.

In the midst of all of this, I still held firm God existed, Jesus came to save us and there was a Holy Spirit. One day my faith was challenged. A girl in my grade five class cornered me by the coat rack. She wanted me to start swearing and doing the things the other kids in my class were doing that I knew were wrong. I told her I couldn't because I was a Christian. Then in a mixture of vulgarity and disappointment she asked if I could stop being a Christian. Believing I would be a Christian for the rest of my life, I told her no. I hoped she would accept Christ, but she didn't want to give up all the things she was not supposed to do.

Unfortunately, it was not long before I too started doing the things I had once known were wrong. I was convinced there was nothing wrong with trying to contact the dead through Ouija boards. I was taught you didn't even need to have a store bought board. You could make your own out of paper if you knew where everything went on the Ouija board. So I made a lot of Ouija boards at school. I would try and talk to spirits all the time asking them whatever came to mind. I didn't really believe the boards worked though. I always thought someone else was pushing the triangle.

A few months later, my class was taking a health unit that included a section on sexual abuse. The teacher encouraged us, to tell a person we trusted, if we were being sexually abused. She gave examples such as mom, dad (these were obviously out of the question), teacher, friend, pastor or anyone else we trusted. I contemplated this for awhile, but felt I had no one I really trusted. I always believed, for some reason, if I told anyone what happened, they would not believe me. My dad was involved in one of the local churches and was produce manager of the largest grocery store in our city and I was just a child. I was afraid I would never see my family again or everyone would hate me for ruining our family. In the end, I decided to remain quiet.

On the last day of the school year my friend Marsha came over for a sleepover. We often had sleepovers and I always wanted to go to her place where it was safe. If we were at her place then my dad could not sneak into my room at night. I had learned to avoid him fairly well during the day, but it was impossible at night.

Marsha had been over for the day and eventually it was time for bed. She slept on my bed and I slept on the floor between the bed and the wall. Eventually, after much laughter and picture drawing on our backs, we fell asleep.

There was a thunderstorm that night. The rain was falling heavy and the lightning was flashing. As the thunder was crashing, all of a sudden I woke to find my father's hand in my pants. As I opened my eyes, his genitals were in my face. I abruptly sat up. As I did this, I saw his naked body run out of the room swiping his hand across the back of my friend who was oblivious to what had just occurred.

Frightened and feeling all alone, I just sat there in the dark. What was I to do? Secretly I hoped Marsha had seen everything he had done to me so someone would believe me. I peered out my window to watch my father peel out of the driveway in his red pickup truck never knowing where he went that night. As I sat there in the darkness trying to figure out what to do, I decided to wake my best friend in the whole world and tell her what happened. I knew deep down even if she didn't see what happened, she would believe me and maybe even know what to do.

It was very hard to wake her up. As the streams of tears slid down my face, I pleaded with her to wake up. Just when I thought there was no hope of waking her, she started to talk. I told her everything that had happened. She encouraged me to go tell my mom. I was too afraid to tell her myself and so I made Marsha promise me she would come with me.

We quietly crept into my parent's bedroom. My dad was still not back yet. We shook my mom awake. I told her my dad had been in my room with no clothes on. She asked me where he was and I told her he left in his truck. She then told me not to worry about it and to go back to bed. I was heartbroken and confused. The last thing I was able to do was go back to bed! (My mom obviously did not fully grasp what I was trying to tell her.) Marsha and I decided we would stay up instead.

Marsha and I went into the kitchen and made tea and rice crispy squares. She just sat there and talked with me. At one point she had me laughing so hard, a piece of rice crispy shot right out of my nose. We laughed even harder after that. From there my memory fades.

As time went on, we no longer attended church and the thought of Jesus was sporadic at best. I would take Him "off the shelf" as it were, when I felt I needed Him. A relationship with Jesus was no longer a concern or a desire for me. My prayers were empty prayers, often just pleas of escape. In addition to all this, I soon began hanging around with a very tough crowd at school.

By the time I was in grade six, I began smoking frequently at what we called "The Cancer Corner" or the "CC". I will never forget that very first drag…the girls kept saying I had to try it. I tried coming up with a ton of excuses, but none of them were very convincing. Eventually, I caved and took my first drag. As I inhaled, it was as if I could feel whatever purity I had left leave my body. I felt so disgusting inside, so dirty and I couldn't take it back. The girls were all pleased with themselves because "Little Miss Goody-Two-Shoes" had done something bad. The CC was within eyeshot from my house and yet that didn't seem to stop me either.

Sinning, after that, became easier and easier. I had already blown what I considered my purity. What was one more step closer to hell? Wasn't I already living in it? I might as well get the best out of it. My dad started giving me alcohol. We had made a silent pact; I could take beer out of his fridge as long as I didn't tell my mom. Fair enough I figured. My friends would often sleep over and we would get totally plastered in my room. I would steal a pack of my mom's cigarettes, some bottles of booze and head down to my room. I thought I was somehow blessed because I had a lock on my door and could get away with practically anything. My dad, however, could still unlock the door.

Pretty soon I began lying non stop about anything and everything. I lied to protect myself and at other times I lied for no reason at all. The lying got so bad I barely knew the difference between a lie and the truth.

One night I came across a box of magazines that belonged to one of my older brothers. I took the box into my room and started going through it. At the top of the box were boring car and guitar magazines. For some reason I kept searching the box thinking there would be one magazine I would be interested in.

As I started getting closer to the bottom of the box I found something I was never looking for. At the bottom of the box was a bunch of pornographic magazines. I started flipping through the pages. I knew I should not be looking at the pictures, but I couldn't seem to stop myself. The more I wanted to stop the more I wanted to keep looking. I saw things no child should ever see. I now knew what sex was without a doubt. Anything that was supposed to be beautiful about "making love" had now vanished from my mind. The nakedness of the people looked different than I had supposed they would. There was something alluring with how they dressed and what they were doing. With eyes wide open I saw what was dirty, violent and the most dangerous part was it became more addictive with each page I turned. However, after that night I never wanted to see pictures like that again. I was disgusted with myself and felt completely dirty.

My self image was incredibly tainted and damaged. I thought if I could just find the right look then everyone would like me and my dad would stop hurting me. Eventually with mindset, I became anorexic. I weighed 95 lbs and still thought I looked fat. To my dismay, I soon realized it didn't matter what color my hair was, if I was fat or skinny, or if I looked ugly, beautiful or sexy- the reality was the abuse was never going to stop!

One day my parents sat me down and told me I was exhibiting attention seeking behaviors and it needed to stop. Trust me when I say, "If someone is seeking attention it is for a reason- they need the attention for one reason or another". Please do not dismiss attention seeking behaviors. My parents wanted me to answer for why I was acting the way I was. My dad knew why, but what was I going to say? So, I said nothing. Fear, anger and hatred began to rise in me.

It was time to start grade seven and I knew I needed a game plan. This would all just become a memory if I could manage to survive the next ten years. I decided I was going to finish school as quickly as I could, and leave the country. Europe seemed a perfect place to move to.

I challenged the school to upgrade me from grade seven to grade nine justifying the move with the fact I had been in the TAG (Talented and Gifted) program for 3 years. I had also already begun, and had almost completed, the grade seven math textbook over the summer. The principal said a flat out no, because it had never been done in our school system before. I fought the system all the way up to the superintendent. After months of fighting, I met with an educational psychologist who preformed an IQ test. I passed with flying colors. I then met with the principals of the local high school. They said if I completed the core grade eight subjects, through correspondence, before the fall of grade nine, then I could go straight into the high school. The first part of my plan was working.

I went to school during the day, studied the grade eight courses in the evening and snuck out and got drunk at night. My marks were straight A's and B's in all subjects. I worked hard for my freedom. Upgrading meant there would be one less year of abuse. My dad still molested me often, but I was blessed with very little memory of it. I would often get so drunk I would pass out and remember nothing at all.

Through my drunken stupors and studies, I managed to start dating guys as well. I had my first kiss by the age of twelve and had multiple boyfriends by the time I finished elementary school. I had my first really intense relationship during my grade seven year. We would sneak out, get drunk and then make out in front of all of our friends. What did I care? They knew we were together anyway. Why keep things secret from them? I had enough secrets in my life as it was.

When we would sneak out, there were only a few places we would go. We would break into the apartment buildings across the street from my house. We'd go into the back loading dock where the garbage was stored and drink back there. Sometimes we would break into the mailboxes, read the people's mail and then throw it all over the building. I would on occasion feel guilty for the vandalism, but not enough to stop doing it.

Some nights we would go to Jacob's house. His dad was a single parent who worked the night shift. We spent many a night getting completely hammered and smoking up a storm. We thought it was a lot of fun to see who could pass out first and then we would humiliate the person. We'd either color all over them with permanent marker or spray shaving cream all over them. I was often the only girl at the party. This brought a sense of pride because I could keep up with the boy's alcohol consumption.

Still yet on other occasions, we would go underneath the local bridge that went across lethal waters. One night it was pretty cold, so we decided to take aviation gas from the gas line beside the bridge. There was enough gas in the line to fill a jerry can. We put the jerry can at the bottom of one of the pillars under the bridge and then we all stood back. One of the guys threw a match into the jerry can. There was such a huge explosion. God must have been watching out for us that night because no one died. My shoes caught on fire and burned until there was almost nothing left. There was a massive black mark on the cement pillar under the bridge for over a decade. Unfortunately, this wasn't the only criminal activity that night. One person from our group also stole a quad and went joy riding until the police caught him.

The nights when it was warm, we would just walk around town drinking. I had told my friends about what was happening at home, but they couldn't help either. The best they could do was just keep sneaking out with me.

The lines between what was right and wrong had become totally blurred. I enjoyed the rush of sin which was tangled in fear. I craved the high from the fear of getting caught. How far could I push the envelope? I would soon find out. Eventually I was caught and my window was nailed shut. There would be no more sneaking out for me.

Fear rose deep within my soul. How was I going to protect myself during the night? There was a blower heater behind my bedroom door. The location of the heater was in an awfully convenient location. I could sleep in front of the warmth of the heater and keep my dad from getting into my room as well.

Overjoyed that I passed my correspondence courses, I went on to high school. I hadn't been in the school for more than a few weeks when I got into my first of many fights. A girl came up to me from nowhere and cut off a piece of my hair. Naturally, I started swinging. To my pleasant surprise the principal suspended her and not me.

Most of my teachers liked me and I did well in my classes. Now that I was in a new school, friends were easy to come by. I hung around with the popular crowd who also drank very heavily, partying almost every weekend. Boyfriends changed frequently. And to top it all off, I attended all of the school dances either drunk or had alcohol stashed outside.

The dark secret of abuse eventually separated me from meaningful friendships and any kind of freedom. Believing alcohol was my only true friend, I spent a lot of time in a bottle. It was no surprise that I was on a one-way street headed for destruction.

*The eternal God is your refuge,
And underneath are the everlasting
arms.*
~Deuteronomy 33:27~

Knocking at Death's Door

Who is waiting for death, but it comes not; and dig for it more than for treasures? My face is reddened from weeping, and on my eyelids is the shadow of death...
Job 3:21 & Job 16:16 MKJV

Some people say death is an easy way out. I thought it was the only way out. The only problem now was how was I going to do it?

Coming home from school one day, I told my mom my health teacher had given us an assignment about over the counter drugs. I told her at some point I would need to gather all the pills in the house and write down what we had. She bought the story hook-line-and-sinker. I was so proud of myself. All I had to do now was to wait for the right moment.

A couple days went by and I learnt my parents were going to be getting the keys for the new house they had just bought. I figured this was going to be the best time to go through with my plan. My parents wouldn't be around to stop me. I wasn't worried about my brothers either, not that I recall why.

It was a few days before my 14th birthday and I remember how warm and sunny that day was. The sun shone in the kitchen window as I reached on top of the fridge to grab every pill bottle I could find. I gathered a huge container full of prescription and over the counter drugs; everything from chewables to prescriptions with warning labels. I searched the house high and low making sure I had found every possible pill. There should have been enough medication in the house to do the job.

After my parents left, I went into my room, locked my door and sat on my neatly made bed. As I sat on the bed I began to open each container reasoning that if God in fact was real, He would have mercy on me because I couldn't live with the abuse anymore. I convinced myself even if God wouldn't forgive me, hell would be better than this. This kind of thinking was completely wrong. Hell would be much, much worse and there is never a way out!

Slowly, one by one, I laid each pill out on the bed. I sorted the pills out by size, color and whether it was chewable or not. All I thought about, in that moment was I would finally have peace and no one could take that away from me. I had heard in my health class, people who were contemplating suicide always reached out for help first. The teacher also gave all of the warning signs of what to look out for. I took a mental note of all of these things and made sure I did not exhibit any of these warning signs. I didn't want anyone's help- I simply wanted to die.

With a large pitcher of water and a glass beside me, I counted each pill as I took it. After taking the 364th pill, I grabbed my blanket and pillow, turned on my heater and curled up in a ball behind my door. (I am not sure why I never left a note that night. I don't think it even ever crossed my mind.) I began to fall asleep with the hopes I would never wake up again.

Not knowing how much time had passed, I woke up with extreme pain in my stomach. It burned something fierce. I ran to the washroom and began throwing up. Fear set in and I didn't know what to do, so I ran upstairs and called the hospital. I told the nurse on the other line what I had tried to do. She asked me if my parents were home and I explained to her where they were and how there was no way of getting a hold of them. She then asked if there was anyone close by who could take me to the hospital. I told her my uncle lived next door and might be home. The nurse told me to stay by the phone because she was going to try and get a hold of him.

A few minutes later I was with my uncle. I will never forget how loved I felt in that moment. He walked me across the yard and into his car. He put his arm around me and I felt safe for the first time in years. In a soft and gentle voice, he asked me why I would do such a thing. In my drugged up state I tried to tell him what my dad was doing to me. Things went fuzzy for a while after that.

The next thing I knew I was in a hospital bed with someone telling me to swallow. The person was shoving a tube down my nose and into my stomach. It was the most awful feeling. A very large nurse came into my room and leaned over my bed to tell me my parents were on their way down. I was petrified. What was my dad going to do to me? Now I really didn't want my uncle to leave.

The nurse asked me what kind of pills I had taken and how many. After telling her I had taken 364 pills, she told me I was going to have to drink a whole lot of charcoal. So, bit by bit I began drinking a cup of charcoal. The taste was not too bad but the texture was awful. It was like swallowing mouthfuls of gritty sand. After I would swallow some charcoal, I would throw up. The nurse asked me why I wanted to commit suicide. After telling her everything my dad had done, I begged her not to let my dad into the room.

Waiting for my parents to show up, I examined the room I was in. It was cold and white, very sterile and boring. The only thing to really do was watch the clock. My parents soon arrived and my mom came into the room. She did not seem too happy with me. She asked me why I had tried to commit suicide. Awkwardly, I told her it was because Dad was molesting me, at which she asked me who I had all told. I don't remember what was talked about after that, but by the morning I was no longer telling the truth about why I had tried to commit suicide. So I recanted and said I lied because I was mad at my dad and the real reason I tried committing suicide was because a boy at school was terrorizing me.

Everyone bought the story. My mom took me home in the morning and sat me down in the kitchen. She asked me what I wanted her to do. She said she would divorce my dad if I wanted her to. I think my mom was scared too. One thing was for certain; I didn't want to be the reason the family broke up. I didn't even want my dad to leave; I just wanted him to stop. My mom cautioned if I told anyone what had happened, my dad could lose his job. In reality, there weren't a whole lot of options for my mom either. Now that I myself am a mother, I have begun to understand the dilemma my mother must have been in. First and foremost, this was a lot to take in. Her child had just tried to commit suicide claiming it was because of the father. We were also a foster home with girls who claimed a whole assortment of things, some of which were true and some were not; she must have wondered if this was what I was doing. Not to mention, the thoughts of what if I wasn't lying, how would she support us kids and what would people say? I would also think it would be safe to assume this would all be accompanied with a great deal of pain and confusion.

By the time I got to school that afternoon everyone knew what I had tried to do. The guy who was getting pinned for my suicide attempt was in my class. I told him what I told the authorities and then apologized for blaming him knowing he might get into trouble. He told me not to worry about it.

After class, I was called down to the counselor's office. I told the counselor my big whopping lie and he too believed it. Afterwards, I went outside with some of my friends. We sat out there smoking for the rest of the afternoon. I didn't know what I was going to do now. I needed a new plan.

Over the next year, I started hanging out with tougher and tougher crowds. Knowing I could have almost any guy I desired, I became addicted to the power this had. Not to mention, I was incredibly flirtatious with every male regardless of how old he was. I could get guys to do almost anything I wanted. I could get them to buy me alcohol, drugs, cigarettes, and even get them to beat up other guys for me.

Darrel was one male friend of mine who I was very fond of. He was the only one I was not willing to date because I knew what I would probably do to him; I didn't want to hurt him. Darrel would do practically whatever I asked him to. He was incredibly tough. For a tall skinny guy, Darrel was probably one of the toughest guys I knew. His dad worked at one of our local hardware stores. His parents spent a lot of time out at the lake and I would sometimes go out to visit. Even in later years I would stop in to say hello.

One night I ran into Darrel outside one of the gas stations. There was a group of guys who were harassing me and wouldn't stop. I asked Darrel if he could take care of the problem for me. He then walked right up to the guys and punched the one who was saying the most, square between the eyes and broke his nose. I felt honored and superior as a woman. That one action fed my need for power more than I realized.

Now at the age of fourteen, life continued on as what I called normal. My dad continued to get progressively worse, as did I. The more vulgar and frequent the abuse became, the more I drank and snuck around. I often lied about where I was going and who I was going to be with. It was almost guaranteed wherever I was going, I would be drunk and with a guy. I was never single for very long and there was a vast array of good looking guys for me to choose from.

I felt a false sense of security in constantly dating. I was a tough girl who was often in fist fights. I had no problem wrestling with the guys either. No one would have believed I was actually a walking ball of fear. I constantly walked in terror. I didn't feel safe out in the world and felt even less safe at home.

*Be strong and courageous. Do not be
terrified; for the Lord your God will
be with you wherever you go.*
   ~Joshua 1:9~

The Dream

And it shall be in the last days, says God, I will pour out of My Spirit upon all flesh. And your sons and your daughters shall prophesy, and your young men shall see visions, and your old men shall dream dreams. Acts 2:17 MKJV

Usually my dreams were terrifying and would wake me in a cold sweat. I was often running or being chased in my dreams. Whoever or whatever was chasing me never could be seen, but I knew it was closing in on me. I would always try to scream but nothing ever came out.

One night, however, when I was fourteen, God blessed me with a strange dream. I dreamt about my future husband. The man I was going to marry was going to bring me a single red rose and a teddy bear. In the same dream, I dreamt my mom and I were going to be pregnant at the same time.

The next morning I woke up and shared my dream with my mom. We had a good laugh about it. My dad had a vasectomy so they were definitely not having anymore children. We both thought it was a funny and strange dream. Then a few days later my mom invited me to go out for lunch with her and her good friend I called Aunty Sandy. As we sat eating our lunch, my mom started giggling. Between the giggles she asked me to share with Aunty Sandy the dream I had earlier in the week. I told her my dream and then we all had a good chuckle. The dream seemed so far fetched and totally impossible.

And Jesus looking upon them said to them, "With men this is impossible; but with God all things are possible."
~Matthew 19:26~ ASV

Enough Is Enough

For you spent enough time in the past doing what the gentiles like to do, living in sensuality, sinful desires, drunkenness, wild celebrations, drinking parties, and detestable idolatry. 1 Peter 4:3

Surrounded by fear, rage, and addiction, I found a new group of friends. This group was feared in school. I found them just to be misunderstood. They were all people from dysfunctional homes where love was replaced by abuse. None of us knew what to do with ourselves or our situations. So we drank heavily, smoked plenty and raged on anyone who got in our way.

I got into a lot of fights in the 10th grade. I fought with my brother, cousin, friends and strangers. Anyone who looked at me crossways or said something I didn't like. Amazingly enough I was only suspended one day in the entire year. The one day I was suspended was because I got into a fistfight with a family member in the middle of the school. The principal wasn't even upset. He said I was to go home and watch soaps all afternoon with my mom, which was exactly what I did. It wasn't until recently I really began to understand how wrong it was to have dishonored my cousin by fighting with her.

By this time, the actions and words of my dad had become more and more vile and perverted. He would say things to me like, "If only you weren't my daughter I'd marry you". I would think to myself, "What difference does that make? You do what you want to anyway." At that time my mom traveled to conferences every once and awhile. One time while she was on a trip, my dad pinned me against the stove in our tiny kitchen and told me I had to be the mom now and do all the things a mom does. He then let me go, but not before his hands caressed my chest.

Up until that point most of the abuse happened during the middle of the night while I slept in my bed. Slowly he began to show me his genitals during the waking hours. My dad would leave his zipper open on his pants or wear really short shorts and then hang himself out and walk around the house like that. He started doing this in front of my friends as well. I rarely invited anyone over once I realized what he was doing.

My dad's drinking got heavier and heavier. One weekend when my mom was out of town, I went to a house party and came back loaded. My dad was sitting on the living room couch waiting for me (he too reeked of alcohol). When I walked in he was holding a hair brush. He told me he wanted to brush my hair. The last thing I wanted was for him to touch me. I pleaded with him to let me just go to bed. I told him I was too drunk and needed to pass out. Adamantly, he told me I could go to bed after he brushed my hair. He pulled me onto the couch and made me sit between his legs. He was erect and hanging out of his pants. As he brushed my hair, he rubbed himself in between the couch and my butt. Eventually, I broke free from his grasp and ran to my room. I locked the door behind me knowing he had a key to the door. I was so loaded I just wanted to go to sleep. He started scratching at my door and meowing like a cat. I was angry and terrified at the same time. My stomach started to hurt and I flung open my door, ran past my dad who was on the ground on all fours like a cat and burst into the bathroom. I vomited, rinsed my mouth and then left the bathroom. When I opened the door, my dad was nowhere around. Back in my room, I locked the door and shoved a knife into the door frame so he couldn't get into my room. Within seconds I had passed out cold.

The beginning of grade eleven rapidly approached and I started to spin out of control. As soon as school started, I started dating a twenty-one year old drug dealer and I was only fifteen. Night after night, I said no to drugs as I watched others do mushrooms, acid, cocaine, meth, weed, and hash.

Near the end of September I started formulating a plan of action- I had resolved to kill my father. However I was going to kill him, it needed to be undetectable, until it was too late. Whatever I was going to do, I had to make sure he couldn't turn it on me. This ruled out a lot of possibilities. Finally, I decided I was going to take a sheet of acid and put it in his coffee. By the time he realized what had happened, he would either be dead or so messed up he would never be able to hurt me again. Either way, I was going to be free from him. The time was coming soon, very soon.

As I waited for the day to come, he continued to molest me often. Finally, one day he asked me to pour him a cup of coffee. This was the moment I had been waiting for; however, I didn't have the acid. So I searched the cupboards to try and find something lethal. Eventually, I found a bottle of cough syrup with some sort of warning label. I poured the entire bottle into his cup and then filled it with coffee and milk, hoping he wouldn't notice the taste. With the cup of coffee in hand, I slowly walked over to him. The sun was penetrating through the living room windows as I handed him his cup of coffee. He took one sip, then spiting it out, exclaimed it was awful. He asked me what I had put in it. I told him I must have put too much sugar. With all hopes deflated, he told me to make him a new cup. I never tried to kill him again.

Enough was enough. I couldn't die, I couldn't kill him, and no one ever believed me or stopped him. What else could I do? Back to the drawing board…

Back at my boyfriend's apartment, four of us made a pact. Three of us were going to run away and hideout at my boyfriend's. My parents weren't going to know where I was because they didn't even know who I was dating. I changed boyfriends so often I didn't think they could keep up.

A few weeks later, on Thursday, October 14, 1993, my grandparents came over to visit. I saw this as an opportune time to take off. My parents would be busy for hours talking with them and wouldn't even notice I was gone until the morning.

My bedroom was in the basement, so it was going to be easy to crawl out my window and take off. I packed a bag, pushed open the window and slowly crawled outside.

The sky was dark and clear. There were thousands of stars in the night sky. It was beautiful, but eerie and cold. For a city, there seemed to be silence in the air- dead silence. I slowly crept along the side of my house and when I got past viewing range, I ran like I never ran before. The snow was deep and my shoes were not adequate for the weather. As I cut through the school yard, it seemed as if I could hear what the people in the houses were saying about me. I felt like they all knew I was running away and they were mocking me. With every passing car I thought the driver knew who I was and I was going to get caught before I ever made it to my boyfriend's apartment. I ran for about ten blocks, barely stopping. The only time I would stop running was if a car was coming, so I didn't draw attention to myself.

Eventually, I reached my boyfriend's building and ran straight inside. I opened the door to his apartment, jumping directly into his arms declaring, "I did it!"

That night was the very first time I got high. Everyone else had gone into the apartment across the hall and I was alone with my boyfriend. He convinced me to try weed. He thought it would help me to relax. I laughed for a very long time after getting high. Then the munchies came. I could not believe the insatiable hunger which followed the high. In no time, like all my friends, I too was hooked on drugs. However, I didn't need to buy or sell for my drugs, because I got whatever I wanted from my boyfriend- the dealer.

Morning came way too early. There was a pounding on the door, around 7:30 in the morning. We all shot up knowing my parents were at the door! One of my friends helped me into the bathroom. He closed the door behind us and locked it. He opened the window and helped me crawl out. I had no time to grab a jacket though, and it was cold. Meanwhile, my boyfriend was answering the door and I could hear him telling my parents I wasn't there. My parents told him they knew I was there. He argued with them at the door giving me enough time to escape.

I ran through the backyard, jumped over the fence and ran across the elementary school yard, as fast as I could. I was about five blocks from my high school. Fear had so gripped me that the winter's cold bite didn't even bother me. I ran down the streets and then down a huge hill and up the other side. At the top of the hill was the parking lot to my high school. Without stopping, I headed for the back doors.

To my dismay, the doors were locked because of how early in the morning it was. I was cold and scared. I knew I didn't have much time to get into the school before I was caught outside the doors. I started banging on the doors like a wild child. Surprisingly, for how large my school was (1200 students), it didn't take long for the janitor to come and let me in. I hid in the school until my friends showed up. It wasn't too long before my parents were also in the school and they brought the police with them. My friends helped me hide behind corners, so I didn't get caught. I didn't know what to do. One of my friends suggested I go down to the counselor's office and tell her what was happening. At this point I had nothing left to lose.

My friend James came downstairs with me, to make sure I safely made it into the counselor's office. As I sat at her desk, I knew for some reason, I had to tell her almost everything!

I sat in counselor Karen's office all morning telling her the horrors of my life. She was listening and I knew it. Karen said she was going to call Child and Family Services as well as the police. I told her I would only agree to it, if I could live with her at her house, at least for a couple of days. I didn't trust other foster homes because my parents knew most of the foster parents. If I was placed in a regular foster home, it wouldn't be long until they knew where I was. I needed somewhere safe to go, some place where they would never look to find me. Karen promised she would do everything she could. She then picked up the phone and told the person on the other line, "You better get down here quick. There is a major disclosure happening in my office." I then heard her say, "The police are already here looking for her. They are in the school with her parents." Lunch soon came and my friends brought me lunch from the cafeteria. Not too long after lunch, the arrangements were made and I was going to my counselor's house. The agency called it a "safe house".

An hour and half before we were to go to her house, a moment in history happened not only at our school, but also in our city. A small plane crashed across the street right into a house. The plane took out the power lines causing a complete blackout in the school. I was instantly terrified because I could not find my counselor and I didn't know where she lived. How was I going to find her in the dark? Praise God it wasn't too long before we were connected. School was immediately dismissed as a safety precaution. I was relieved we were leaving the school and I would be safe, at least for a short time.

A week had passed, since I had left home and I missed my siblings very much. I wondered how they were, hoping the agency was going to remove them from our home also. Anticipation began creeping in because I knew my little brother Jonathan was going to be at the high school in a couple of days. The next Thursday was high school for the junior high kids. I waited outside the room all morning. Jonathon was in there and I desperately wanted to see him. I needed to know if he was okay or if my dad was taking my leaving out on him. .

The class was dismissed and out walked my little brother. I was so excited to see him. I just wanted to hug him so bad. When he saw me, he did something I never saw coming. He took one look at me and walked in the other direction. I called for him at the top of my lungs, but he wanted nothing to do with me. I had lost the one person in my life I not only loved, but trusted. Now I trusted no one.

Disclosing what happened to me had come with a high price tag. At this point I wasn't sure if it was worth it.

From the fullness of His grace we have all received one blessing after another.
~John 1:16~

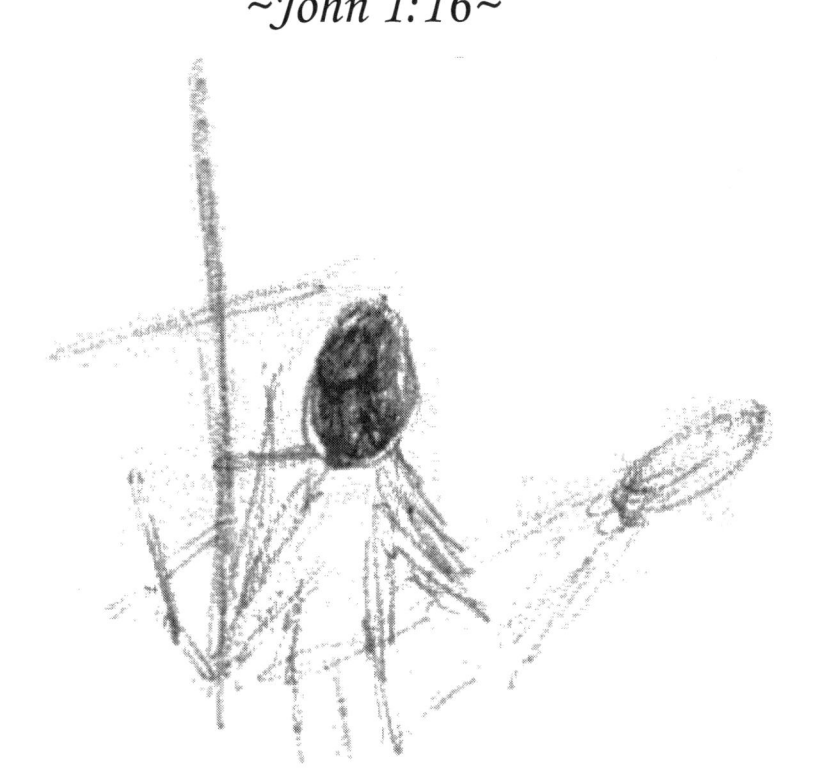

Crossroads-On The Brink Of No Return

He shall return no more to his house; nor shall his place know him any more. Job 7:10 LITV

Colder weather rapidly swept across the city. I enjoyed the comforts of my counselor's warm home and kind family. Karen had been gifted with the arts. She could draw and paint beautiful pictures. I often examined her artwork as I danced around their home. Unfortunately, a warm and loving home was not enough to save me from myself. I took advantage of my counselor's kindness and hospitality. On that same token, my boyfriend was taking advantage of my vulnerability. There was one night we got intoxicated and then started to make out. He wanted to take things to the next level. I wasn't so sure because I had never "been with" a guy before. On the other hand, I really didn't want to lose my virginity to my dad. With this in mind, I figured it wasn't really that big of a deal. I was really nervous and a bit scared because I had heard your first time hurt a lot. So, at fifteen years old, in a run down drug house, I lost my virginity to a twenty-one year old man.

After losing my virginity, I realized I had found a whole new high. Not only could I get a quick fix in the bedroom, but I had discovered a new way to control a man. There was power in that room and I wanted more of it.

A week or so later, a friend of mine came over. We thought it would be a good idea to play with a camera. The pictures started out funny at first. Slowly though, the pictures became sexual in nature. By the time the film ran out, we were taking pictures almost completely nude. We took our pictures in to get developed and couldn't wait to get them back. Once we got them back, we were pretty impressed with ourselves. I thought I would make a good centerfold. I gave one of the pictures to my boyfriend as a keepsake.

I continued to drink, do drugs and stay out all hours of the night. My physical appearance had changed quite drastically too. One day I shaved half of my hair so I had only a little ponytail on the top of my head, my clothing was seductive and I was frail.

Not long after moving into the safe house, I was told I needed to meet with a psychiatrist. I knew once again, no one believed me. The psych evaluation was to see if this guy could figure out if I was lying about my dad or not. Once in the room, I told the psychiatrist everything that had happened to me. I even gave him intimate details, in hopes he would believe me. To my dismay, he thought I was lying. The irony was, I had lied about so many other things in my life, it felt almost strange to tell the truth. Everyone believed a liar, but no one believed the truth.

After leaving the room, my head started spinning. It felt like I was about to lose my mind. I knew I was on the brink of no return. I went home to rest and by the morning I was functional again.

My boyfriend and I broke up and were not on good speaking terms. I was told he and another dealer were competing to see who could get the most virgins. I wanted revenge! This caused dissention in our group. I wanted everyone to hate him too, but was not successful. He supplied the drugs and I didn't.

A day or two later, my ex was yelling at me outside at school, so I figured this was a really good time to get back at him. I yelled at the top of my lungs in front of about 300 people, "Yeah, well, you were no good in bed anyway!" There was a ton of laughter. I then stormed into the school. At the next smoke break, a so called friend of mine, walked up to me and pushed me into the snow. She started punching my face, but it didn't hurt even a little bit. I was laughing, because the snow was so soft, my head just kept sinking in the snow. It would be like trying to punch someone under water-not a whole lot of impact.

Eventually, I got fed up and kicked her in the face. A teacher pulled us apart hauling us into the office.

We were asked why we were fighting and I told the principal I didn't have a clue why; I thought we were friends. She, eventually, apologized explaining how she was paid by my ex to try and beat me up. I looked at the gash under her eye and giggled thinking he had just wasted his money.

Life was really starting to crumble. I lost my boyfriend, I no longer had free drugs, no one in my family would talk to me, and to top it all off, I was told the agency was moving me to a group home called Merry Mound North. I begged and pleaded with my counselor to let me stay. I was petrified about going into Merry Mound; only the worst of the worst were sent there. It didn't matter what I said, that's where I went.

I moved into Merry Mound a few days later and realized it wasn't as bad as what I had thought. The workers were really nice people and I knew most of the kids who were living in Merry Mound. Because I had dropped out of school, the workers told me I had to do correspondence in the home. This seemed like a reasonable request.

Not everything came up roses for me though. The girls could sometimes get really mean. One night, I was arguing with one of the girls and she yelled I was just my daddy's little sex toy. Without thinking, I whipped my brush at her, but missed. When it hit the doorframe it broke into two pieces. We all started laughing and the fight was over.

One afternoon, we were all watching a popular talk show. My teacher was on the talk show. His daughter had falsely accused him of sexually abusing her. She had apparently been brainwashed in therapy through hypnosis. This did not help my case at all. Everyone thought I too had falsely accused my dad, even though I knew he was molesting me. I told everyone who was watching, I had not lied and some day, I too would be on a talk show, and then they would believe me.

I was living in Merry Mound one of the first times I got arrested. My friend Jennifer and I were AWOL (Absent With Out Leave) from Merry Mound, in other words, gone without permission. We were found in the mall which we both thought was a really funny place to get arrested. The cop asked us not to run because they really didn't feel like chasing us. We agreed not to run. We were placed in handcuffs and escorted out. I quickly realized I could easily slip my hands out of the cuffs. I slipped my hand out and motioned for my friend to place the cuffs up her sleeve. Finally, when we were about to get into the car the cop realized we were no longer cuffed. My friend and I started laughing at the cop and then got into the car. We were placed in the holding cells until our workers came to pick us up.

Secretly I was tired of living this life of drugs, promiscuity, and alcohol. One day I broke down and told the workers I wanted to change my life around. There was a school dance that week and I figured this would be a good way to start over. I used to always go to the dances.

Just as I got to the dance, a car pulled up with a bunch of girls who I knew were incredibly unpredictable and dangerous. They asked me if I wanted to go with them. I told them no, I just wanted to go to the dance. The next thing I knew I was in their car. I didn't know what was happening. I thought they were just pulling a prank on me. Boy was I dead wrong. When they let me out, they took me into the basement of a house. They sat me in a chair and wouldn't let me move off of it. They forced me to drink a lot of what I thought was beer. My memory from that night is foggy at the best of times; it fades in and out. I believe not remembering every thing is probably a blessing.

There was this one girl there who everyone called a he-she. I wasn't sure if she was a guy or a girl. I soon found out she was a girl. The other girls wanted me to have sex with her. I told them I could never! Then I started to notice there was something terribly wrong with the beer. I didn't feel just drunk, I felt high too. In a desperate attempt to escape I told them I had to go to the bathroom. They were not going to let me use it. I told them if they didn't, I was going to go right in my pants and all over the floor. Reluctantly they let me go to the washroom.

While I was in the washroom, I knew I needed to figure away out. Suddenly I got the urge to run. I opened the door to the bathroom, ran straight up a flight of stairs and out into the frigid night air. I just ran and ran. I didn't even stop to look back. I ran halfway across the city not knowing where I was going. Eventually, I started walking aimlessly around the main drag. I was wearing summer shoes and a t-shirt. My jacket was back at the house I had been trapped in. Even though it was cold, I was so stoned and drunk I did not notice the temperature. The fact I did not get frostbite was a pure blessing.

As I was wandering in the streets, with no coat on, in the middle of winter, the police picked me up. They asked me were I had just come from. Not believing my story, they laughed at me. I was serious and they told me to quit lying. They said they would only believe me if I filed charges. I told them if I filed charges, the one girl in particular would kill me. They then called Merry Mound to tell them they found me, but I was intoxicated. I then heard the police say they were going to put me in lock up for the night. I could hardly believe my ears. I was the one who was kidnapped and drugged, yet I was going to be the one arrested!

When we arrived at the cells, a cop was waiting to question me. I thought he was one of the cruelest people I had ever met. He and another cop started calling me vulgar names- such as slut. When asked what my name was, I retorted he could look for himself (he had my ID in his hand). It didn't take long for the situation to escalate. The harassment was getting worse and the one officer was manhandling me quite roughly. I was furious, mouthy and rapidly becoming out of control. One of the two cops pepper sprayed me and started laughing. My face burned like someone had poured acid on it. As I screamed, I looked at him, completely enraged, and spit directly in his face. At that point, he bent me over and kneed me. I was then thrown into the cell where I screamed for hours. The burning would not stop. Eventually, I went into my own little world banging my head against the bars and the cement walls. The cops eventually came back into my cell, tied my legs and arms up with packing strips and put a helmet on my head. Once they left the cell, I slipped the helmet off with my feet and continued to bang the back of my head against the bars. Finally, I passed out.

The next morning, I was released into the care of my worker. She asked me what had happened and I told her everything I could remember. There were a few fuzzy spots, like not knowing how I got to where I was, when the cops picked me up. She asked me what happened to my face, so I told her. After hearing about my night, she took me up to the hospital and had an investigation file opened against the police. Months down the road, both officers were forced to apologize to me and were then transferred.

So much for making a new start…

I had given up all hope so I went back to drinking and doing drugs. One night while really drunk, I fell asleep at Jennifer's, boyfriend's house. During the middle of the night, her boyfriend crawled into bed with me. He unzipped his jeans, pulled down my pants and slipped himself into me. I didn't know what to do, so I did nothing. I cried through the entire thing.

A few days later, three of us girls, from Merry Mound, got together to make a pact. Jennifer, Stacy and I were going to runaway to Florida. I was going to pimp Jennifer because we believed she could make us enough money to make it to Florida. We were going to live on the beach and live off the land, maybe even get jobs if we had to. But first we needed to figure out how we were going to get enough money to get on a bus. We decided to steal a checkbook from Stacy's mom. As soon as we had the checkbook, we wrote a fake check for five hundred dollars. We cashed it and bought our tickets. At the last minute, Jennifer backed out. That was ok, we figured we would be out of the country by the time anyone realized we stole the checkbook. We'd figure the money thing out later.

Stacy and I hopped on a bus and headed for Winnipeg. When we got there it was late at night. We realized we had nowhere to sleep, before we left the city in the morning. I called one of my brothers to see if we could stay with him, but his wife said no. I then called an old boss of mine and she said we could stay, but only for the night. She came to pick us up from the bus depot.

The next morning, we went to a store and bought some pocket knives. We figured we needed something to protect ourselves with. After buying the knives, we left the store and started walking down the street. All of a sudden, I heard my name being shouted. I hesitated, not wanting to turn around, but I did anyway. I had to know who was calling me. It was one of my older brothers. I could not believe he found me, in a city with half a million people in it. Somehow he convinced us to go out for lunch with him and our oldest brother.

We went to a pizza joint. My brothers were trying to make conversation, when two very large cops walked into the restaurant. They were there for us. It was baffling how my own brothers set me up! Stacy and I were arrested and placed in the back of the police car. I was really hungry, so I asked if we could take the pizza with us. I was shocked when they said we could. While we were sitting in the back of the car, I realized we still had the stolen checkbook. I needed to figure out a way of getting rid of the checkbook before we got searched at the station. There was a crack in the seat of the car that perfectly fit the checkbook. The cops asked us if we had any weapons on us. We admitted we both had pocket knives. They asked us why we had knives with us, so we told them we bought them incase a guy tried to jump us. The knives were confiscated. Strangely enough though, the cops weren't disturbed about the weapons. These two officers were probably the nicest police I had ever met. Any fear I had of them quickly faded.

Once in the holding cell, we were told we were being sent home on a plane. Stacey and I sat in the cell for a few hours with nothing to do. Therefore, we decided to amuse ourselves by singing. We sang as loud as we could. As we were laughing, an officer came into the cell smiling. He told us to keep it down because people were not supposed to be happy in jail. For a change, we decided to do as we were told. A few hours later we were on a massive jet headed for home. I had only been on a plane once before when I was really sick as a young child.

Back home nothing had changed. I became more and more out of control. I wanted to change, but couldn't. I figured if I moved to another town it would be easier. I wanted to move to Churchill where I couldn't run and no one knew or had heard of me. My worker told me she would try and make arrangements. While I waited, I continued going AWOL.

One night, a bunch of us from the group home, stuffed our beds to make it look like we were sleeping in them for room check. We jammed the outside door earlier in the day, so it wouldn't automatically lock. We did that so we could sneak back in without being noticed. I never thought there would be a problem. I thought I had planned the escape route and everything else really well. Exiting and entering were covered, so was room check. I never thought they would notice us gone. I was wrong.

In the middle of the night, the cops found me at a house party. I was very drunk and more than likely stoned. After being arrested, I was placed in the holding cells. In the morning, I asked when I was going to be let out. I was told I wasn't going to be let out. It was freezing cold in the cell. I was only allowed to keep one of my shirts and neither of them was warm. I had no socks either. In total, I spent ten days in the holding cell. Over the course of my stay, I became very sick and was loaded with cold sores. Not wanting to use the washroom in the cell I tried not to eat anything. I knew there was a camera in the cell and the thought of them watching me go to the bathroom totally creeped me out. The couple of times I had to pee, I took a blanket and wrapped it around myself. The first time I did that, the officer on duty asked me what I was doing. Rudely I replied, "Going pee!" There was one older lady who worked behind the desk who took pity on me. She gave me a pair of socks and a blanket. I was not permitted to shower the whole time I was there either, which probably made the skin infections worse.

While in jail, my parents came to visit. They brought me a couple of oranges. I had never appreciated fruit like I did in that moment. I wanted all this to end. I was sick, scared, tired and weak. I just wanted to go home and have my old life back, even if it meant getting sexually abused. After a decade of abuse, what was three more? By the end of the visit with my parents, I decided to recant. I told the police and the agency how I had lied about the whole thing. I just wanted to go home. Again, I was believed when I lied. They told me I would not be able to go home right away because I was being sent to Churchill. I was okay with that. Churchill was where I wanted to go in the first place. I needed to clean up and get my life back in order.

Things started out really well in Churchill. I quit doing drugs, got a job at the library, went back to school and had a couple of decent friends. The group home I was living in was really good. I loved the workers. The only thing I didn't like was how cold it was up there. It was often -60°C or colder with the wind-chill.

I hadn't been living there for long, when I started dating. As usual, the relationship didn't last very long. My longest relationship lasted around three weeks.

One day, I went out on a skidoo with one of my friends. The sun was incredibly bright out. You could hardly see because of the reflection off the snow. We were driving behind the complex, when we ramped off a huge snow drift. We had the skidoos practically full out. There was no way we could stop our skidoos from smashing into the brick wall. Both of us were unconscious for a few seconds. When we came to, we asked each other if we were okay. Miraculously we were both just fine. I had a triangle missing from the three layers of pants I was wearing and the skis were bent straight up at a 90° angle. Other than that everything was completely intact.

Before long, I again crashed in life as well. I could not get away from my reputation. I started scrapping and hanging around with the tougher kids. Smoking, drinking and doing drugs became a part of my everyday life again. One night, I stayed over at my boyfriend's house with his sister Rachael. While we were drinking in her room, she pulled out a Ouija board. We then tried contacting the spirits. This seemed a little different than the paper ones I made as a little girl. I started wondering if there actually was life beyond death. As Rachael and I played with the Ouija board, we were answered by the demonic. I don't really remember what we asked or what the response was, but I do remember feeling an unsettling feeling about the whole thing. We eventually put the board away and went to bed.

Shortly into my relationship with Rachael's brother he began using me for sex and I wanted revenge. One afternoon, her brother and I went and bought a bottle of vodka and drank it up in his room. In a slow hushed tone, I convinced him in his drunken state that I was actually from another planet. I told him if he didn't stop taking advantage of girls, I was going to seek revenge on him. I started to actually creep myself out while talking to him. He believed me and was scared of me after that.

Life in Churchill started to crumble very quickly afterwards. Before long, I went home for a visit which drastically changed my life.

You live in the midst of deception; in their deceit they refuse to acknowledge me, declares the Lord.
~Jeremiah 9:6~ NIV

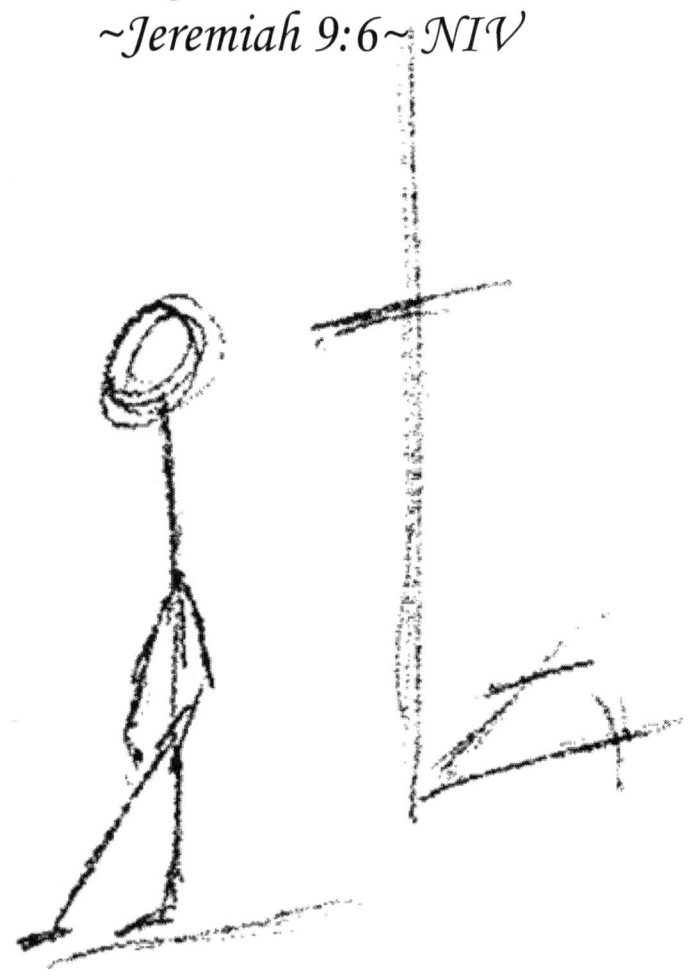

Beginning of the End

How long, O Lord, must I call for help, but you do not listen? Or cry out to you, "Violence!" but you not save? ...be utterly amazed. For I am going to do something in your days that you would not believe, even if you were told.
Habakkuk 1:2 & 5 NIV

$\mathcal{H}$ome seemed liked such a foreign word to me now, but that's where I was headed. The date was now February 19, 1994; and I was only fifteen years old. I had just gotten off of the plane expecting to see my mom, who was supposed to have picked me up. Instead my dad was there alone, waiting for me. Fear gripped me as my stomach began churning in knots. Waves of panic began hitting me as I thought about the long drive from the airport to my house. Like a sheep headed to the slaughter, I followed my dad to the station wagon. Before leaving the airport road my dad turned to me with contempt in his eyes, he told me he was taking a real chance picking me up like this. He was implying I would make up some sort of story to get him into trouble. I didn't say a word. I just sat there trembling. Deep down I knew there was something terribly wrong, but could not discern what it was.

Later that night, my dad's lawyer came over to the house. My parents were upstairs visiting with the lawyer when I decided to go to bed. The wood stove was on in the rec-room making it nice and toasty warm, so I tucked myself onto the couch. Sleep had not quite whisked me away when my dad came into the rec-room. Fear took a hold of my heart causing it to start beating a million miles per minute. Slowly I could feel the fabric of my shirt begin to move as my dad leaned over the back of the couch. He began lifting up my shirt to expose my chest. As he started moving his hand across my breast I rolled over pretending to be disturbed in my sleep. To my relief he left the room and went back upstairs. I started freaking out. What was I going to do? I had nowhere to run. I told everyone I had lied about him abusing me and I thought for sure no one would believe me now. However, something in me told me to go upstairs and tell his lawyer what had just occurred. I didn't know what I was going to say. It took every ounce of courage I had to just sit up on the couch, never mind go up the stairs. Slowly I got to the top of the stairs, walked through the kitchen and into the living room. In a timid, yet angry voice, I declared, "He just did it again!" My mother and the lawyer both stopped talking to look at me. My mom looked confused and asked me to repeat myself. So with more courage and anger I repeated, "He just did it again!!!" They both knew what I was talking about. My mom told me to go back downstairs into my little brother's room. In obedience I turned and headed back downstairs. I jumped onto Jonathan's bed with him and told him to be very quiet. A few minutes later, my dad, in a drunken state of rage, came bursting into the room. I don't remember what he said, I just remember being terrified and screaming. I can't remember who came downstairs (either my mom or the lawyer) and got him to leave the room. Sounds of screaming and yelling could be heard all throughout the house. From where I was I could not hear what was being said, so I snuck to the top of the stairs. Just as my dad was leaving the house, I heard my dad attempting to blame my mom for his actions. There is very little else I remember from that night.

By the time I woke up the next day, my dad had left town. My mom had the RCMP stop him approximately four hundred kilometers away to bring him back. My mom, who I did not get along with at the time, suddenly became my hero. She was bold and fearless! She had him come back to the house to confront him with me. To my relief, he confessed to everything. Finally, the truth was out and a thousand pounds lifted off of me.

After the weekend was over, I went back to Churchill. An appointment was made with my worker and I told her what happened. The worker called my mom to inform her I was saying my dad had molested me over the weekend. This time my mom sided with me and told the agency I was telling the truth- my dad had molested me.

A few weeks later, arrangements were made for me to move back in with my mom. It didn't take long to settle back into my old room. Life was going to be better now. The nightmare of my life was over- or so I thought.

And I will multiply men and beast on you, and they shall increase and be fruitful. And I will make you dwell as before, and I will do better to you than at your beginnings. And you shall know that I am Jehovah.
~Ezekiel 36:11~ MKJV

I Have Loved You Since The Day I Conceived You

Sanctify all the first-born to Me, whatever opens the womb among the sons of Israel, of man and of beast. It is Mine.
Exodus 13:2 MKJV

Realizing the abuse was over gave me hope for a new start at life. I really wanted to be different. I wanted to change and just live a normal life. After living the way I had, I thought it would be easy to stop now that I was home. With everything in me, I was going to try to go back to the way I was- respectful, peaceful and drug free. Life was going to be good now. All I had to do was live.

One bright, winter morning, my mom sat me down in the living room. She explained to me she had something to tell me. Then she told me she was pregnant. My dad had a vasectomy, so when I asked her how this was possible, she confessed he was not the father. This somehow strangely made sense to me. Not only did it make sense, but I could hardly contain my excitement.

A few weeks later, the father of my mother's unborn child moved in. Jonathan and I both really adored this man. My little brother and I immediately wanted to call him dad. We craved for the love of a father. I didn't know what it was like, but imagined it would be wonderful. To my pleasant surprise, he was (and still is) an amazing father.

At this point in my life, I was not in school and had no intentions of going back anytime soon. My time was spent skiing and hanging out with a group of new, but older friends. Greg, a guy who was eight years older than me, came skiing with us one time. He seemed nice and was a lot of fun. Greg and I started to see each other more and more. He was big into the party scene and to my dismay, drugs as well. Within a few days of dating Greg, I started doing drugs again.

My new dad was concerned when he found out I was dating Greg. One day my parents invited Greg over to nail him with a barrage of questions. My dad asked Greg questions such as, "What are your intentions with my daughter?", "Do you love her?" I was thrilled, angry and confused. It was awesome my dad was standing up for me, but why was he doing this? What were my *dad's* intentions? I wasn't sure how to feel about the situation. I was pretty sure this is what "real" dad's did for their daughters, but I had never experienced it before.

One afternoon, while I was cuddling on the couch with Greg, it dawned on me maybe he was the one I was going to marry. Foolishly, I told him about the dream I had how I would know who my husband was going to be. He just looked at me and smiled. A couple of weeks later we started fighting and broke up.

Prom was just around the corner, and I really wanted to go, especially to the parties. If I had not dropped out of school, I would have graduated that year. I would have graduated a couple of days after my sixteenth birthday, which was only two months away. To my delight, a friend of mine knew of someone who still needed a date for prom. I barely knew the guy, but a day or two later, he asked me to go with him to the prom; I was thrilled.

Prom was not everything I dreamt it would be. The parties afterward started out as a lot of fun. I walked into one house party where there were a couple of grade nine girls puking in the toilet. I laughed at them, calling them losers, for not being able to handle their liquor. By the end of the night, I was so drunk; I passed out on the lawn. Vaguely, I remember throwing up outside. (There is a tad bit of irony there.) The next day, I woke up in a house I had never been in before. What a frightful mess I was all covered in grass and dirt. As I slowly peeked through the cracks of my eyes, I figured out I was in my prom date's basement. To my horror, my jeans were undone and I started freaking out. With a tone of accusation, I asked my date why my pants were undone. Almost laughing, he told me to calm down. He quickly explained I went to the washroom and could not get my zipper done up. He then went on to tell me, I then promptly passed out on his couch. What a relief! A few minutes later, he drove me home.

I was feeling a bit sick all week; nothing major though. I had never been that drunk before, so I wondered if I had given myself alcohol poisoning. Time went by and I felt better again, but realized I never got my period. I wasn't too worried, although I did tuck the thought into the back of my head.

A week or two later, I was at a house party where everyone was getting hammered. I decided not to drink, just in case I was pregnant. Greg called the party wanting to talk to me. As soon as I grabbed the phone, Greg began apologizing for being a jerk and wanted to be friends. I informed him he had better start being a lot nicer to me because there was a pretty good chance I was pregnant. He immediately told me he was coming to get me. With great indifference, I reiterated, I was going home to bed. After hanging up I headed straight home. Greg followed through and arrived at my parent's house shortly after I got home. I was thankful my parents told him it was too late to see me and sent him on his way.

A week or so later, I went to the doctor; I was pregnant. I went straight home and just stood in the bathroom for what seemed like forever. Slowly, I placed my hand on my stomach. I could hardly contain my excitement; I was going to be a mom. This baby would love me! The thought of someone always loving me unconditionally was almost too much to imagine. With both hands on my belly, I whispered to my baby, "I have loved you since the day I conceived you."

Within a day or two I needed to tell someone I was pregnant, but I was not ready to tell my mom yet. So, I told the next best person- Aunty Sandy. I went over to her house and told her I was pregnant. She asked if I had told my mom yet or not. I squirmed when I thought about having to tell my parents. Sandy offered to come with me to break the news. I figured she would be a good buffer, so I gladly took her up on her offer.

I sat both my parents down and told them the news. They were pretty disappointed in me. They asked me what my plans were. All I knew to answer was I was not quite sure yet. The only thing I was sure of was I needed to get back into school right away. We called the school and I was able to get back into all the classes I had dropped out of first semester. That part was kind of neat because I picked up almost exactly where I had dropped off, which made transitioning really simple.

It took me about a week to work up the courage to call Greg. I explained we needed to talk because I was pregnant. We went for a walk to talk about what we were going to do. Greg wanted me to abort, but I told him abortion was not an option. As we were walking down the street by my high school, a red van pulled up. It was his parents. They told us to get in. I was incredibly nervous. The last thing I wanted to do was to talk to his parents. His mother accused me of ruining her son's life. I questioned that by reminding her Greg was twenty-three and I was only fifteen. I stormed out of the van and started walking home.

Not too long after finding out I was pregnant, I began spotting. My doctor sent me for an emergent ultrasound. While getting the ultrasound, the technician pointed to my baby; all I could see was this tiny little dot. Even though my baby was only a little dot, I still thought seeing her was pretty cool. Everything was fine. The bleeding was just from the baby attaching to the uterus. I was thanking God.

About eight weeks into my pregnancy, I started freaking out. I wasn't sure if I was ready to be a mom. The father of my baby quit talking to me and wanted nothing to do with me or the baby. And to top it all off, people were trying to convince me to abort the baby. I didn't toy with that idea for too long before I decided abortion was definitely not an option for me.

Time passed and I started considering adoption. I thought about it on and off throughout the summer. If I was going to go the adoption route, I wanted Aunty Sandy to adopt my baby. As time went by though, I started to fall in love with this baby growing in my womb. This child I hadn't even met consumed my thoughts and heart; I loved her very much. In my eyes, this baby had saved my life. I went back to school; got a job, quit drinking and doing drugs. I had a whole new set of friends I loved and adored and who in turn treated me like gold. By the time I was five months pregnant, I decided to keep the baby and no longer considered adoption an option.

Mid pregnancy, I learned my blood type was RH- and I needed to find out the blood type of the father. My mom tracked Greg down and explained to him how my baby's life could be in danger depending on what his blood type was. She asked him if he would go and get tested. We were all relieved when he said he would be willing to go and get tested. He was RH+ which meant I needed to get injections so my body would not reject my baby.

After going for another ultrasound, I was then sent for what I thought were regular monthly ultrasounds; the doctor would later tell me she was concerned about the health of my child. It was pretty neat being pregnant at the same time as my mom. I will always cherish her willingness to come to most of my appointments to share the experience with me.

Our bellies began to grow and soon it was time for my mom to have her baby. It was really exciting because we knew she was having a girl. My mom went into premature labor and had a beautiful 3lbs 12oz baby girl. It was quite easy to fall in love with my baby sister. I loved to hold and rock this tiny, beautiful bundle of joy. Often I would just sit rocking her on top of my ever increasing stomach. Sometimes the babies would kick each other and I would laugh. We were all pretty sure I was having a girl also and looked forward to the bond the two girls would have. I didn't have any names picked out yet but we were all getting tired of saying "it" or "baby" so my dad suggested we should call her Wilma. This was a pretty funny, yet a very clever idea- Wilma it was!

Being able to see the movements of my unborn child during the ultrasounds was amazing. Wilma was the cutest thing ever. While staring at the black and white screen in complete awe and wonder, she began clapping her precious, tiny hands. What an amazing sight. She was the most beautiful thing I had ever seen.

The time was getting closer for me to have my baby. I thought out of respect for my child I would try talking with Greg again. We went out to my favorite pizza joint and just talked. It went really well and we decided to get back together. We spent a lot of time together before the baby was born. One night while over at Greg's friend's, Greg made a comment which struck fear into me. He was joking around with his friend when Greg suggested to him if my baby was a girl than his friend could "have" her, as in sexually. I firmly replied, "Over my dead body". The guys laughed. I was ready to go home.

Time had passed and I was now overdue and very ready to have this baby. Greg would take me for speed walks and rides in his truck down bumpy roads; all to no avail. I started wondering if this baby was ever going to come out. My original due date was on my mom's birthday in January which came and went. Seven days later was my brother Jonathan's birthday. This day too came and went. Then on the twenty-second of January Greg called me to say there was always a two percent chance the baby was not his. He then told me he wanted a DNA test. This not only hurt me, but enraged me also. After hanging up the phone, tears fell for hours. I curled up on the living room couch and just sobbed. My parents tried everything they could to console me, but I eventually cried myself to sleep.

The next morning was the first day of my final exams. I shot up at 7:00 am thinking I was peeing myself. It didn't take me long to figure out my water had just broke. Running upstairs as fast as a pregnant girl could, I went to wake up my parents. My mom tried to encourage me to try and rest a little more knowing

I was going to need it. I, however, was way too excited. One of my friends came over a little later in the morning and stayed with me the whole day. She was also pregnant and due shortly after me. Eventually the pain became so unbearable I needed to go to the hospital. However, we had to wait for my dad to get home from work first. By the time he got home I could barely walk. He helped me into the back seat of the car and drove me to the hospital. It seemed like he was driving a million miles per minute, so I told him he was driving too fast and begged him to slow down (seems pretty funny now looking back).

As soon as we got into the hospital, the nurses tried to put me in a wheelchair. There was no way I was going to even attempt sitting. Burying my face into my dad's chest, I clenched my fists around his jacket holding onto him as tightly as I could. Tiny little baby steps was all I could take walking down a very long hallway. After many small steps, I finally made it into the room where I thought I was going to have my baby. The nurses hooked me up to monitors and got an IV going. Originally I told my dad he could come to the hospital, but I didn't want him in the room with me; I changed my mind. He tried to leave me and I would not let him go. There was no way he was leaving me now. Not only was he my focal point, but I had myself convinced I could not breathe without him.

A few hours later I was in heavy labor. The pain was like nothing I had ever experienced before in my whole life. I had not taken prenatal classes and had no idea what to expect. If you have never given birth I will save you the details, but be sure there was searing pain involved!

A few hours later I was moved into the birthing room, where I realized something was wrong. The doctor was having a hard time keeping track of the heartbeat of my unborn child. The doctor called in a specialist to probe my baby's brain which is where they stick a wire into the baby's head to keep track of the heartbeat. There seemed to be a lot of people in the room. Exhaustion overtook me so the birthing team had to keep waking me up and telling me to push. Finally at 11:27 pm I had a beautiful baby girl in my arms. Tears of joy flowed as I looked down at her. A nurse came to take her, but I didn't want to let her go. My parents assured me I would get to see my baby after she and I were both cleaned up. My parents were amazing coaches. My dad held my hand and breathed with me. My mom rubbed my back and told me when my contractions were coming, peeking and ending. I felt so blessed they had shared this experience with me.

That night I tightly held my baby falling madly in love with her. It was hard to believe how much I loved her. I never knew you could love another human this much. She was perfect in my eyes and I thanked God for her. The name I gave her means *The Lord's* or *Belonging to the Lord*. A few hours had passed when the nurses wanted to take her back to the nursery, but I was adamant my baby was staying with me.

The next day I filled out a sheet of paper for who I did not want coming to visit me and my baby. Greg and his family were placed on the list. A little while later a nurse came in and told me my baby needed to go for an ultrasound on her brain. I didn't understand why. The nurse didn't know no one had told me there might be something wrong with my baby. Immediately I called my mom crying while trying to explain what I was told. A moment or so later the nurse came back to take my daughter for her ultrasound.

There had been fluid on my baby's brain which was the reason why I had so many ultrasounds when I was pregnant with her. The ultrasound measured the fluid on her brain. To my relief she was going to be okay. Her fluid levels were on the high end of normal. If there had been anymore fluid she would have needed a shunt in her brain.

Over the course of the next three days my daughter and I had a lot of visitors. As much as I loved the attention both my daughter and I received, I was looking forward to taking my baby home to start our new lives together. Even though I could not afford to buy a crib I was quite comfortable with her sleeping with me. In fact I had no desire to put this precious child down.

When I got home, my parents told me to take my baby downstairs and unpack. When I got into my room there was a beautiful white crib set up with bedding and everything. Overcome with joy, I started crying. I knew my parent's didn't have much money and this was a beautiful brand new crib. Overwhelmed with gratitude, I wasn't sure how to thank my parents enough so they would know how much I appreciated what they had just done for me.

I loved my new life. I had two parents whom I loved, a drug and alcohol free life and a beautiful daughter I wanted to live for. Change had to be permanent now, it just had to be.

Is it possible for the skin of the Ethiopian to be changed, or the markings on the leopard? Then it might be possible for you to do good, who have been trained to do evil.
~Jeremiah 13:23~ BBE

False Identity

*The godly may trip seven times, but they will get up again.
But one disaster is enough to overthrow the wicked.
Proverbs 24:16 NLT*

I once believed your identity was defined by what you did or who you were dating. After having my daughter, I found my identity in being a mother. My identity soon changed from mother to finding my identity not only as a mom, but also wrapped up in who I was dating. I would suffer from this false identity for close to a decade.

My baby was about six months old when I started to have a crush on a guy named Daniel who I had known since the ninth grade. He was not like any of the other guys I liked before. He was quiet and respectful. I had been in classes with him on and off throughout high school. Strangely enough, he had never caught my attention before. We were in the same math class together and I wanted to talk to him but was too shy.

Finally one night, I worked up the courage to call him. I was trying figure out what kind of excuse I could use to talk to him. What would he think of me, considering I had a baby and all? I finally came up with the perfect excuse. I was going to call and ask for help with my math. I dialed his number, let it ring twice, then chickened out and hung up. Within about a ten minute time period, I did this several times.

At last, I let it ring long enough for someone to answer. I then promptly hung up. Taking in a couple of deep breaths, I called again this time I spoke. Daniel answered! Immediately, I began to stutter through asking about a math question. We ended up talking for quite a long time. He then started giggling and I didn't know why. So I asked him what was so funny. Daniel then let me know he had call display. Now you have to remember call display was a new thing and I didn't know anyone who had it. I was mortified! We had a good long laugh about my foolishness that night.

Weeks went by and we started talking more and more. Our desks moved closer and closer together as well. By spring we were dating. I had never been in a long term relationship before. It was so strange and new. It didn't seem like his dad approved of the relationship very much at that time. Sadly, Daniel's dad was also a single parent and I thought he would have understood my situation.

Before I knew it, I was madly in love with Daniel and could think of nothing but him. One day, Daniel came over with a red rose with greenery and baby's breath in it as well as a truly unique teddy bear. There was a big bear attached to a smaller bear and on the smaller bear's shirt was the head of a baby bear. We would say the big bear was Daniel, the one attached was me and the head was my baby. I thought for sure he was the one I was going to marry. This seemed to be the fulfillment of my dream. After all, the first part about my mom and me getting pregnant together had come true. To top it all off, Daniel was very romantic and would write me beautiful poetry to sweep me off my feet. Daniel, my daughter and I had become very close, spending all of our free time together.

Unfortunately, I really had not changed as much as I had thought...

Daniel was a virgin when we started dating, but I soon robbed him of that. The relationship then became very intense. Being intimate was practically all we did. Almost all of my firsts were with him. I remember thanking God for him. I believed with everything in me we were going to get married. We talked about it on and off all year. He had never really been in a relationship before and I had never been in one this long. I loved Daniel as much as I loved my child. Just the thought of him would tie me up in knots. There was nothing I wasn't willing to do for him; I would have gone to the ends of the earth for him if he had asked me to.

My past now seemed like a distant memory even though only a year before I was being molested by my dad, hooked on drugs and practically living on the streets. Now I had a daughter, a dad who loved me and a man I believed loved me as well. Every one in our graduating class would say if anyone would make it past high school it would be us. It was like a Cinderella story come true and Daniel was my knight in shining armor.

Even though things had been rough for me in the past, I knew almost everyone in grades eleven and twelve; probably close to eight hundred people out of the twelve hundred in the entire school. I got along with almost everyone and had been in almost every crowd at one time or another. When we got together almost no one knew who Daniel was. When I would say who I was dating, people would have no clue who I was talking about. He had a small, close group of friends he had grown up with who for the most part stayed out of the limelight. I thought it was pretty cool he did not have a reputation and thus no one really knew him.

In the spring, we went to prom together and to my delight, Daniel was voted prom king. It was an amazing night. I looked at him with awe and wonder. How did I wind up with such an amazing guy? He loved not only me, but my daughter as well.

Prom quickly came and went and so did our school year...

My birthday was a couple of days before graduation. Daniel took me out to the lake where we had steak and wine on the beach. We spent the whole weekend in each other's arms. This was what I had always imagined love would be like. Sheepishly I asked Daniel what my baby was going to call him when she could start talking. He reassured me I wouldn't have to worry about it because we would probably be married by then. Then he spoke the words I had been hoping for- "Daddy would be just fine." He took my breath away when he said that.

Daniel's brother came home for our graduation and told him when he moved out to Thunder Bay he would find him a "real woman". I was deeply crushed. This was the last family member for me to meet and he totally disproved of me. I loved their mom and their dad was slowly starting to warm up to me. My heart wondered if his brother knew how much I loved Daniel maybe he would have thought differently of me. Even though I was relieved when his brother went back to Thunder Bay, worries began to cloud my thoughts.

The summer was coming to an end and Daniel was moving to go to school. We both cried for most of the week. I must have known this was the end because I told him when we were both forty and divorced he was to call me. Pain shrouded our chuckles through streams of tears. The day finally came and Daniel left. The stress of him leaving gave me the second worst cold sore I had ever had in my life. I couldn't even kiss him goodbye.

The only thing I could do was cry for the next week straight. I just held my baby and wept bitterly not knowing what to do with myself. Every waking moment in the last eight months was spent with Daniel and now he was gone. Inside, I felt totally empty and grieved.

My good friend Georgette tried to cheer me up while keeping me company. I was so grateful for her in my life. She would constantly remind me it was only going to be a few weeks before I would see Daniel at Thanksgiving. This was not as comforting as she thought though. I had a really hard decision to make. My grandmother, who was dying from cancer, was coming up for Thanksgiving. Even though I loved my grandmother more than she would ever know, I chose to go to Thunder Bay to spend Thanksgiving instead. Daniel told me we were going to look at rings when I got to Thunder Bay. The thought of looking at wedding rings had me so twitterpated that I chose Daniel over my grandmother.

My daughter and I got on a bus to meet Daniel in Winnipeg. I could hardly wait. When the bus pulled in he was there waiting for me. I ran into his arms and just like in the movies, he picked me up and swung me around. It felt so good to be in his arms again. As he kissed me passionately it was as if my entire body had melted in his arms. We drove all night and pulled into Thunder Bay as the sun was just coming up.

It was nerve racking going to his place knowing how Daniel's brother felt about me. With all of the tension, it wasn't long before we started fighting. Within two days, Daniel and I got into a huge fight. Daniel yelled it was over. I was so confused. I told him I couldn't believe I had wasted my time on him when I could have been at home with my dying grandmother. That was the clincher. He left the apartment and I desperately wanted to go running after him. I asked Daniel's brother if he would watch my sleeping baby, but he said no. I felt trapped. Going after him wasn't an option and I definitely didn't want to be in there with his brother. With much anger and frustration, I went back to his room and sobbed. Daniel finally came back and I thought we were going to be able to work things out but we couldn't. We both cried on his couch and the next day I left. I knew I had not only just lost the man I loved, but I was losing my best friend as well.

Grief stricken, I got on a bus the next morning and cried the whole way home. I was so thankful my baby was not only excellent the entire way, but she was there for me to hold. My heart had just been ripped into two pieces which I believed could never be put back together again. Instead of coming back with an engagement ring I came back single and inconsolable.

On the way home, I dreaded the thought of going home having to face everyone. I was mortified and speechless. Praise God, my grandmother just held me tight. She told me Daniel did not know what he had just lost. The comfort in her arms meant the world to me. Not knowing how to thank her enough for her love and support, I took my grandmother out for lunch that afternoon. She had tried to pay for the meal, but I told her I wanted to treat her to lunch. She was extremely special to me and I wanted her to know how much I loved her.

Going back to school was so incredibly hard. I didn't want to look at or talk to anyone. They all expected me to come back with a ring on and to tell them we had split up was too hard to bear. My friends, to their credit, were very sympathetic with me. Georgette took really good care of my emotional needs listening to me babble for hours on end.

The months passed and I would talk to Daniel on the phone on and off. We mostly fought though. One month after we broke up I found out he was dating someone else. The fit of rage I took could be compared to no other. How could he claim to love me and want to marry me and then so easily dismiss me. He had changed a lot after moving in with his brother. He didn't seem like the same guy at all. Even this didn't change my heart though; I still loved him as much as I always had.

Daniel told me he would always love me, but he was no longer "in love" with me. My heart broke more and more with each word spoken. The roots of pain and bitterness sunk very deep into my soul. I would constantly play the weekend over in my head thinking of things I could have said and done differently. Daniel's dad was incredibly kind to me in those days. He would invite me to go for a ride on his motorcycle or would invite me to just pop in. Sometimes, I would take him up on the offer. His kindness helped me through losing his son.

Two months later was Christmas and Daniel was coming home. After discovering Daniel was going to the bar, I desperately began devising plans to get into the bar. I thought if he saw me, had a couple of drinks and then slept with me, then we would get back together. I figured if he remembered the passion we shared he would forget about his girlfriend and we would be back together like we were supposed to be.

Even though I was a minor, I figured I could get in anyway. Sure enough I got into the bar and he was there. My heart was pounding like crazy. Daniel and I danced the slow song that night and I took in every moment of it. He was wearing a soft, red, plaid shirt that smelled of his Preferred Stock cologne. I just closed my eyes and sank my head deep into his chest so I could hear his heart beating. As the song ended, I could hardly let him go. I thought if I let him go I would crumble right in the middle of the dance floor. The night ended and with a heavy heart I left the bar- alone.

Daniel came over to visit a day or two later bringing a Christmas gift for my baby. The weather was abnormally warm that night. The sky was clear and the stars were twinkling. I gazed up at the night sky hoping my prayers of reconciliation would be answered.

After my daughter opened her gift, we went down to my room and slowly we started kissing. It seemed so right to me. This was how it was supposed to be. However, my mom soon came downstairs and we stopped before she got to my room. I was so mad believing my chance of getting back together with Daniel had just been ruined. This was the last I saw of him before he returned to Thunder Bay.

Months went by and the pain in my heart did not weaken. When Daniel and I were together, I made a vow to love him as long as I lived. I knew I would never love another as I loved him because I made that vow with everything I had in me. Even if I tried, I couldn't look at another guy. Every time a guy asked me out, I always said no. The only person I wanted to be with was Daniel. I would wait for forever if that's what it would take.

The snow began melting and the time of the trial against my father was rapidly approaching. I had not seen my father in close to two years. At the courthouse, not recognizing my own father, my mom pointed him out to me. I tried hard not to stare but I could not believe this man was my biological father. He looked so different. The way he dressed, his weight and hair color had all changed. I was in total disbelief.

There were a few people who came to court with us that day. One of the people who came to support me was Constable Roy who had kept an eye on me and would come to visit me every time I was in jail. I had great respect for this man and was grateful for his support. He was one of the few people who had believed me when I told him what my biological father had done to me.

My biological father had made a plea bargain which the courts accepted. Secretly I hoped the judge was going to overturn the plea and throw him into jail for a few years. I wanted him to pay big for what he had done. Also, I knew pedophiles were often treated badly by other inmates and I hoped this would happen to him. Deep down, I hoped he would be tortured in jail or even murdered.

The judge, however, accepted the plea and my father never saw a day in jail. It was a cheap victory. I was, however, able to convince the courts to allow the press to cover the trial and use both my name and my father's name in the paper. I was a minor and at that time they did not print the names of minors under any circumstance. I reasoned everyone in town knew the story, but most people thought I had lied. The next day the title of the article read, "Jeffrey Tomas Sentenced for Sexual Assault." He may not have received any jail time, but at least the truth was out and I thought this truth would set me free.

My wounds are poisoned and evil-smelling, because of my foolish behavior. I am troubled, I am made low; I go weeping all the day. For my body is full of burning; all my flesh is unhealthy. I am feeble and crushed down; I gave a cry like a lion because of the grief in my heart.
~Job 38:5-8~ BBE

Temptations of Babylon

And on her forehead was a name written,
MYSTERY,
BABYLON THE GREAT,
THE MOTHER OF HARLOTS
AND OF THE ABOMINATIONS OF THE EARTH.
Revelations 17:5 MKJV

Summer had once again come to an end and I moved to Brandon to continue my university courses in education. Often thoughts about transferring to Thunder Bay crept through my mind, but nothing ever came of it. I continued to talk with Daniel and his family over the years. The love I had for him never lessened. His brother and I eventually began talking to the point where I would pour out my heart to him, asking if he thought there would ever be a chance to be with his brother again. What a difference from the beginning. Frequently I wondered what would have happened if his brother and father had liked me from the start. I wondered if we still would have broken up. The "what ifs'" and the "why's" plagued me on a continual basis.

David, my oldest brother, and his girlfriend, allowed my daughter and me to live with them while in Brandon. I was ill on a regular basis and often depressed or lonely, which made it hard for me to keep up with my studies. One day while I was at home, I saw a commercial for a talk show and thought I should call and tell them about my life and Daniel and how much he meant to me. When I called there was no answer so I left a message on the machine telling them my whole story and how Daniel's love had saved me from my depressing life. Within a day or two Daniel and I were asked to go on the show. He agreed and we were flown to Toronto. We shared a hotel room and I did everything I could to get him to notice me and desire me. Every female tactic I could possibly think of was used and none of them worked. I wanted to be with him so badly. I believed if we were intimate then we would get back together for sure. Even though nothing happened between the two of us, we had an awesome time together that weekend. He even bought me a beautiful bouquet of my favorite flowers. I had such a hard time believing Daniel didn't still love me. He would say one thing but do another. The weekend was over and we were flown back to our cities. To my dismay, we didn't get back together that weekend like I had dreamed.

It was strange though, I would still see Daniel a couple of times a year when he would pick me up in the city to go home to visit our families. They were very long car rides for me. I thought I was going to explode. A million questions would swim in my mind, but I did not have the courage to ask even one of them. Every time he picked me up he would give both my daughter and I a huge hug. I missed the warmth of those embraces so much.

Christmas would come and go; Daniel always sent Christmas cards. I missed him terribly. I still had not made any friends in the city and never went anywhere. That winter I fell ill for a couple of weeks causing me to get far behind in my studies. My parents offered to take my baby so I could have more time for my studies without having to worry about taking care of a child. It was not an easy decision for me to make, but I thought it was the right one. We didn't say how long because I didn't know how long it would take to catch up. My parents had her for two very long weeks. It didn't take me long to get caught up, but I wasn't able to pick her up right away. That was very painful for me because I missed her so much. It was as if a very piece of my being had been taken from me. What hurt the most was missing her second birthday and there was nothing I could do about it. I cried most of that day. Most of my thoughts circled around the fact that I was such a horrible mother for missing my daughter's birthday. This brief moment in time haunted me for over a decade.

While my parents had my daughter, I went out for the first time in Brandon. I stayed out almost all night with a group of guys from school. We talked about religion most of the night in our university pub. After that night, I started hanging around with them daily. The guys all played with my daughter and she in turn really liked them. To me it felt like being with my brothers. She and I would hang out in the dorms until all hours of the night. I did most of my studies there and began enjoying life again.

My brother David moved to Winnipeg at the end of my first year meaning I had to get a place of my own. Depression hit me pretty hard because I had nothing. I moved into my first apartment with only bedroom furniture. My little one and I ate off of cardboard boxes for the first while. We went from Ritz to the pits. My brother's apartment had a fireplace, 3 bedrooms, a balcony, and was fully furnished. My apartment had only a bed and dresser.

Soon after moving I realized I could not afford the apartment I was in and buy food at the same time. I went broke very quickly. It was in my moment of desperation I cried out to God for mercy. There was no money for food or gas to get my daughter back and forth to daycare. With only half a tank of gas and half a carton of milk, I knew both would run out within a couple of days. Pay day wasn't for a couple of weeks. God blessed me with a miracle. My tank of gas never budged and my milk never ran out or soured. A friend of mine, out of nowhere, dropped off some meat from his parents and I went to a food bank with my daughter. I could not believe life had come to this, but in the same moment I was so grateful to God for the miracle.

It was now two years after breaking up with Daniel, and I eventually got so depressed I stopped caring about what happened to me. The bar became my place of refuge on the weekends where I would dance all night. I never drank at that time because I thought drinking would be totally irresponsible of me as a single parent. However, I didn't see a problem with flirting with the bouncers or any other good looking guy there.

As time went on I started dating, but once again my relationships were very short lived and sexual in nature.

Because of how broke and lonely I was, I decided to move in with my friend Sarah, who was also a single parent. A month or two later, I started dating Sarah's friend Jake who I thought was separated from his pregnant wife. After dating for about two months he asked me to marry him. At this point I figured I was damaged goods and Jake was the best I could get. He also had a lot of issues with drinking and lying. He wasn't even honest about what his job was.

Shortly after Jake proposed to me, I noticed there was something wrong with my body. I had really bad cramps, my discharge was off and I didn't feel very good. I ended up in emergency where a young, thirty year old doctor examined me. He did a pelvic examination and told me I would be called with the results. A couple days later the hospital called to tell me I needed to be treated for Chlamydia. Fury burned deep within my veins! My eyes were beginning to see the truth! I then learned Jake had not actually left his wife at all. I called up my so-called fiancée and reamed him out. As the rage began to build in me, I began taking a hissy-fit in my kitchen, smashing almost every dish I could get my hands on. My roommate took our girls to the basement while I finished my temper tantrum.

When I was done flipping out I decided to plot revenge! I went to Jake's wife and told her everything. She was none too impressed, but seemed to appreciate me coming to her. I told her about the Chlamydia because I was worried she and her baby might have it. She then confided he had given it to her as well, which meant he had been sleeping with at least one other woman. Jake's wife soon left him.

With everything that was going on, I decided to go to the bar one night just to dance my thoughts away. Not too long after being there, my head started to hurt. Being so desperately starved for attention, I went to find a bouncer I liked and told him something wasn't right. I felt high or drunk, my head was pounding and I was having a hard time breathing. As I was telling him this, I collapsed in his arms (partly on purpose). One of the other guys yelled out, "She's just drunk". The bouncer yelled back, "No. She doesn't drink!" At this point they called an ambulance. In that moment I couldn't think about anything else except I wanted to die and my daughter would be better off without me. My roommate, who was with me, kept saying, "Hold on; your daughter needs you". I remember trying to die, but couldn't. I thought if things were truly mind over matter then I could force my spirit out of my body so I could die. The paramedics arrived and tried snapping me out of it. I was slipping in and out of reality. We arrived at the hospital and the same doctor from the month before examined me. This seemingly kind and gentle doctor gave me a pill and then a few minutes later came back to ask me some questions. My memory of the conversation is a little foggy, but I do recall him writing down that I was suffering from depression. I did not want to accept that diagnosis.

A short time later, I had run into the emergency doctor out in a social setting. The details of meeting him are a bit sketchy to say the least, but I do know I wound up at his house and I got very drunk while there. Sarah was with me and made sure I got home in one piece. Then one night the doctor came over to my house. While sitting in the living room, he asked me if I was on the pill. I lied and told him I was. I wasn't sure even why I lied, but at that moment I didn't think it was very important. An hour later he was having sex with me in my living room. He left shortly thereafter. Mixed emotions ran through me about what had just happened. There were conflicting feelings of excitement and violation. I had just been with a doctor; my doctor. He knew things about me no one else knew and to top it all off, I was nineteen and he was thirty. The next day I went and got the "Day After" pill so I wouldn't have to worry about getting pregnant.

It didn't work! I was pregnant once again by a guy who was way older than I was. Looking down at my little girl, I told her mommy had another baby in her tummy. She seemed pretty excited about it. I called the doctor and told him he got me pregnant; he, however, was none too impressed. He wanted nothing to do with me or the baby. I went and saw a prenatal doctor who warned me there could be something wrong with the baby because of the pills I had taken. He went through a whole list of side effects which horrified me.

A few weeks after speaking with doctors, friends and family I killed my unborn child. I told my prenatal doctor I had to do it right away or I wouldn't be able to go though with it. An appointment was scheduled immediately and before I knew it, I was on an operating table removing the life from my womb. After regaining consciousness, I was sobbing uncontrollably and didn't know why. The nurse assured me most women cry as a result of the anesthetic wearing off, but I wasn't convinced the anesthetics were the reason. Almost every female in the room was crying; was it because somewhere hidden deep down inside of us we knew we had just murdered our unborn children? Becoming emotionally numb was the only way I could endure this horrendous experience.

Things had become very dark in my life. Deep from within me I so desired to be a good mother, but I just couldn't seem to get it together. My daughter deserved better than what I was giving her. During my complete mental breakdown, I was seeing dark figures in our house and one night I imagined one of the shadows came off the roof and pinning me in my bed. This was the final straw for me. I loved my daughter so much I was willing to give her away to a good home with two parents who were secure, stable and loving. After confiding in my pastor from back home about what was going on, he told me I wasn't going crazy, but that I was oppressed. I had no idea what oppressed meant, but I felt better blaming something other than myself. He also convinced me not to give my daughter up for adoption. He offered to let my daughter and I live with him for a while so I could get my life back on track. However, my parents persuaded me to not drop out of school. I am so grateful I did not give my child up for adoption. If I had given her up, it probably would have killed me.

My life began taking a toll on my body. I was constantly in and out of the hospital with the most peculiar sicknesses. Crippling pains in my lower abdomen often ended after a heavy dose of IV meds. Sadly though, deep down, I felt relieved sitting in a hospital bed. I didn't have any responsibilities and Sarah had my daughter. It was almost like a paid vacation. The doctors told me I had chronic pelvic inflammatory disease. I would frequently get cold sores also, but on one occasion something strange had happened with one of my cold sores; my lip was swelling. At the hospital, the emergency doctor believed there was nothing wrong with me and sent me home. The next day the swelling was worse and I was not feeling very good. Back at the emergency department, the same doctor was on call. Again he sent me home. Later that night I went back. This time the doctor looked at me with great irritation. He wanted to send me home, but another doctor noticed I was back and came to take a look at me. He was displeased with the other doctor for not taking my cold sore seriously. The cold sore did not stay localized on my lip. It had spread all over my body. Anywhere I had a cut or nick in my skin, a cold sore appeared. There were even cold sores in my eyes. My grandfather said I looked like I had been kicked in the face by a horse. I was placed in the hospital and hooked up to IVs. The doctor came in and told me he was not sure if they were going to be able to get the cold sore under control. He suggested I make permanent arrangements for my daughter. In other words, he wasn't sure if I was going to live. Terrified, I called home to tell my parents what was going on. After a few tests, the doctors discovered all of my vitamins and minerals were almost completely depleted. After many tearful prayers, not only was I feeling much better, I was going to live. What a relief it was to be going home to my daughter.

Time passed and eventually I started dating again. My dating record was what it was before I lost Daniel. I slept with everyone I dated even though my relationships only lasted for three weeks at best. One rule I had was the guys never really were able to meet or see my daughter. No one was ever going to be allowed to love her and leave her again. At the bar I frequented, there was a bouncer who caught my eye. He was ten years older than me and engaged to be married. I didn't care. In my opinion he was still up for grabs. I wanted my pound of flesh and in bitterness, I took my whole life out on every man who came in contact with me. Wrath was filling the hole in my heart.

I struggled badly with wanting to be with Daniel and trying to move on in life. Eventually, I started seeing a counselor. This did not help any. I told her about the dream I had when I was fourteen and how I thought Daniel had fulfilled the second half of the dream. She didn't really counsel me in this or give me any direction on how to get over him. When I realized she wasn't really helping and her office was moving to a different location in town, I quit going to see her.

The affair with the bouncer continued for about a year. The affair ended when I found out I was pregnant. I was pretty sure it was his, but there was one night with an old friend of mine. When I told the bouncer I was pregnant, he freaked out. We promptly quit talking. Rage swelled deep within me; he was going to pay for leaving me. I left a message on his fiancée's answering machine explaining the affair and our unborn child. Didn't she deserve to know what kind of man she was thinking about marrying?

At first I was excited about having another baby, but as I started to tell people, doubts started to creep in and I wondered if having another child was really in the best interests of me and my daughter. Once again I started thinking about abortion.

A couple of weeks later I got a call from Daniel in Thunder Bay. He had heard I was pregnant again and was worried about me. I thought in my mind the baby would have been his if we were still together. It was bittersweet talking to him again. He had been sending birthday and Christmas cards every year to my daughter. That year was the last year he sent her anything.

I soon became very discouraged and at 12 weeks pregnant I killed my second baby. Hours before the abortion, I went for an ultrasound. The technician asked me if I wanted to see the baby. I knew if I looked at the screen I would never be able to go through with killing my unborn child. She couldn't figure out why I didn't want to look at the infant inside my womb. Sadly, in many ways it was easier to kill the second baby. It took a lot less time to rationalize why murdering my child was better than letting it live. The abortion was scheduled to take place about a week before Christmas. After my child had been ripped from my womb, I lied to my family and told them I had a miscarriage. The only love I had left was for a tiny child who was counting on me to take care of her.

My body was soon back to normal and I was as good as I was going to get. It was a new semester and a new year. I decided this year was going to be the year I changed. Dating was going to become a thing of the past and I was just going to raise my daughter and be a good mother to her. I loved her and wanted her to have the best possible life I could give her. This year was going to be the year for change.

All the days of my warfare I will wait, until my change comes.
~Job 14:14~

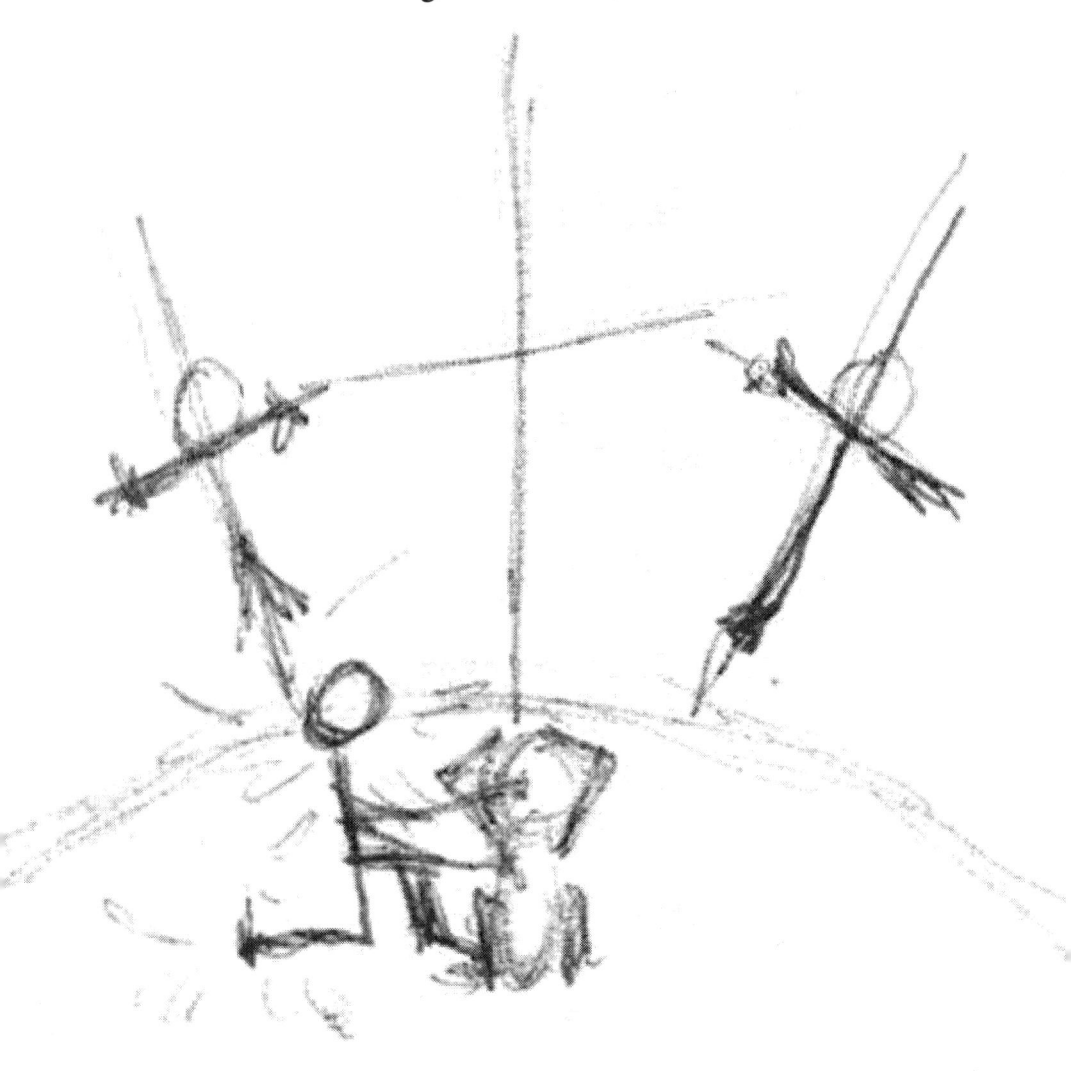

Dream Fulfilled

And since the dream was repeated to Pharaoh twice, it is because the thing is established by God, and God will shortly bring it to pass.
Genesis 41:42 MKJV

The first day back to university was January 5, 1999. Finishing my fine arts minor was required to complete my education degree that spring. I went to my first class and sat down with my friend Andrew. As we were waiting for our class to start, in walks this guy wearing a long trench coat. He swung his coat over his leg as he propped it up on the arm of the chair. He then, in one sweeping motion, brushed his thumb aside his nose and pointed in our direction and said, "Hey Andrew" in a slick voice. I felt embarrassed for the guy and thought to myself this was going to be one very long semester.

Class ended and I went outside to have a smoke before my next class. After the break, I headed into the next building and up the stairs to my next class. To my dismay the guy from the other class was sitting in the room. I could not believe my luck. A person was lucky if he was in the same class with someone they knew, never mind being in the same class with someone twice. After class, this guy asked me if I wanted to go for a smoke with him. Hesitantly I agreed and we went down to our local pub in the university. We sat at a table with a group of people who had been in our first class. I didn't really know any of them. They started talking about horror stories of people's lives. I decided to share pieces of my childhood with them; however, I said the events happened to people I knew. As I was sharing my story, the group just looked at me with disbelief; their unbelief was no real surprise to me. I soon excused myself and went to my next class. Low and behold, this same guy who I now knew to be Marc was in my next class. This was completely impossible. The odds were already astronomical, but to have him in the class after that also was out of this world.

How could this be I wondered. Marc was in all but one of my classes. This was impossible.

After school I went down to the pub to wait for my roommate to pick me up. I was sitting at a table alone when all of a sudden Marc just plunks himself down at my table. I thought to myself, "Who does that?" Marc began talking and joking around; I politely nodded.

Sarah arrived and told me she had made spaghetti for supper. Marc, in not quite a pout or a sing song, but almost a combination of the two, then started saying he was a bachelor, he lived all alone, he had no food in his cupboard and he had nothing to do. In that moment, I noticed not only how cute he was, but how handsome he was as well. Finally, I looked at him and flatly asked, "Marc do you want to come for supper?" He then had the gall to reply with, "I don't know. I'll have to check my little black book." at which he pretended to flip through a book. I hit him on the arm and we all laughed. He came back to the house that night, but he got more than what he had bargained for.

When we got in both of our daughters came out to greet us. I hadn't told Marc both Sarah and I were single parents. We sat down, had supper and a few laughs. I thought Marc was pretty funny. My roommate and I got up to do the dishes as well as a huge soap fight in the kitchen. Then shortly after supper I tucked my daughter into bed.

Marc and I stayed up talking all night. I did most of the talking, however. For some reason I told him almost everything about me. I wasn't sure why I had done that. Part of me was trying to scare him off and I don't know what the other part of me was doing. He just sat there in disbelief. I knew it was a lot for a person who has never met me before to digest. Through our discussions, we soon discovered we had the same group of close friends and yet had somehow never met in three years. This - like the classes- seemed impossible. We were at the same social events, with the same people, and never connected.

We talked until the crack of dawn. My daughter woke up while we were still talking. I then noticed it was morning and all three of us needed to get to school. Marc decided to come with us to her daycare. After dropping my daughter off at her daycare, we met up with Sarah who was also in one of our theatre classes.

With zero sleep, Marc and I had a severe case of the giggles. Our professor was not pleased with us at all. We spent the whole day together and he came back to my house again that night. Again we spent the whole night talking and he fell asleep on my couch. The next morning we took my daughter to daycare and then headed off to our 8:30am class. Again that night Marc came back to my house and we talked until late into the night. We had just spent almost 72 hours straight talking with one another. I had not spent that much time with a man since I had been with Daniel. After I had put my daughter to bed, we started talking again. This time though, we were cuddling on my couch. At one point, I looked up into his eyes and everything in me melted. There was something about this guy I just couldn't get enough of. He looked down at me and then very tenderly kissed me. The feeling was so intense. I had never been kissed like that before. As he kissed me, I could feel his heart pounding and the aroma of his cologne overtook my senses. Something was happening to me I could not explain. We went to class the next day and that afternoon during break, Marc, my friend Georgette from high school and I all went back to my place. After talking for awhile, I pulled Georgette aside and asked her what she thought of Marc. Then in all seriousness, I told her I just knew for some reason this was the guy I was going to marry. Now keep in mind she knew me from high school and knew how many guys I had dated, how long the relationships lasted and how my heart still belonged to Daniel. When I told her I believed I was going to marry Marc only knowing him for four days, she fell on the floor laughing uncontrollably. I kept saying, "shhh" but she couldn't stop laughing. Oh how I dreaded the thought of having to explain to Marc what was so funny.

As I am sure you have guessed by now, Marc and I started dating. To my surprise, it didn't take long for me to fall madly in love with him. I never thought I could ever love another person again. Parts of me felt like I was being unfaithful which was weird because it had been three and half years since Daniel had left me. I pushed the feelings aside and tried to focus on my daughter and Marc.

Not too long after dating Marc, obsession, jealousy and paranoia took over. Fear was the strong man. What if I lost Marc like I lost Daniel? Why did Marc want to be with a person like me; I had nothing good to offer him. He would say he thought I was fun and as long as things were fun he would stick around. Intimacy became a means of power and control. By this point in life I knew what men liked and what they didn't.

One cold winter day, one of our professors pulled me aside demanding whatever was going on between Marc and I had better stop. He was referring to our dating and not our school performance. My grade then dropped from an A to a C in his class which made me furious. I knew the grade was because of personal reasons rather than academics. Marc wrapped his strong warm arms around me, holding me while I cried. He then told me this would be the last time our professor was ever going to make me cry. No one had ever wanted to protect me before. I fell deeper in love with him that night. Marc did many things to make me feel special, which I had not felt in years. One night he held me and sang to me for hours. I felt so blessed and at peace in his arms.

Valentines Day was soon around the corner and I went all out on Marc and my daughter. When Marc came over he surprised me with a teddy bear and a single red rose. He brought chicken for supper and tried making me a cake. He didn't bake the cake long enough and the inside was soupy, but I appreciated it nonetheless.

A few days later I realized what Marc had given me. He completed the dream I had when I was fourteen. He was the only guy to have ever bought me a single red rose without greenery or baby's breath. Now I believed more than ever Marc really was the guy I was going to marry; he just didn't know it yet.

Slowly as time went by we started fighting. The fighting increased and we would break up for an hour and then get back together. This continued and got worse and worse. We had so much passion, we drove each other crazy. In and amongst the fighting was a lot of laughter as well. Even if I was really angry with Marc, he could still make me laugh.

One day after picking my daughter up from daycare, I was driving down the street and as I was turning the corner my daughter looked at me square in the eyes and declared, "Mommy, I want Marc to be my dad." I was stunned and wide eyed. I didn't think she knew him well enough to ponder such a question never mind having the desire to ask him. What was I going to say? The last thing I was looking for was a father for my daughter. This was also the first time she had ever spoken like this. She would sometimes state she didn't have a dad, but didn't seem to be the least bit bothered by it. When she would say this, it was more like a declaration rather than a question or concern.

After taking a moment to think, I finally regained my composure and told her we would have to talk to Marc about it. At four years old, I hoped there was a good chance she would forget about it. I stood corrected! A couple of days later she piped up out of nowhere and looked Marc straight in the face and asked, "Marc, will you be my dad?" Marc started coughing and looked at her and said, "It's not like buying bubble gum sweetheart." That is where the conversation ended.

A month later, the three of us went to BC to take care of my uncle and auntie's house for three weeks. We had a great time there and began to act like a family would. We went swimming in the mountains, played cards, went flower picking and the list goes on. This was the best vacation I had ever been on. After my aunt and uncle returned home, the three of us headed for

Vancouver to meet up with Sarah and her daughter. We all traveled together in Sarah's Geo Metro LSI Convertible which was only a two-seater car. Two adults sat in the seats and then another adult and the girls sat in between the seats and the back window (there was a small space like there is in some trucks to put luggage). After touring Vancouver for a couple of days, the five of us headed back to Manitoba in the Geo. We drove straight home only stopping for bathroom breaks. As we got closer to home, Marc became very irritable. He did all of the driving and a lack of sleep was not fairing well for him. As we got closer to home, Marc and I started fighting quite a bit.

When we finally arrived home, Marc and I broke up a few hours later. Once again, I never saw it coming. Marc told me I had a car full of needs he could never meet. Rage took over and I stormed off home. I figured it had been a long sleepless trip home and Marc just needed some rest. I thought we would be back together by that night or worst case scenario by the next day. To my dismay it truly was over. I tried asking him if he could still see my daughter and then slowly disappear from her life. I was concerned with how traumatized she was going to be with him just suddenly not being a part of her life after spending three weeks straight with him. Marc did not feel comfortable with those arrangements and so I had to break the bad news to my daughter.

When I finally worked up enough courage to tell her, she started screaming and crying. She blamed herself and believed his leaving was completely her fault. I tried to explain to her it was not her fault, but she did not believe me. Her little heart was broken and I wanted Marc to pay for it. Hell hath no fury like a woman scorned!

While at his place getting my things, I blew up in a fit of rage; I saw red. While yelling and screaming at Marc in the hallway, I swung him into the wall pinning him against it. It was as if I had super strength whenever I would get that angry. I told Marc if I ever found out he was with another single parent and he used her like he used me I would kill him. I was completely out of control.

Our breakup drove me back to church for the first time in a long time. I was encouraged by a group of older couples who tried to steer me in the right direction. They bought me a beautiful mom's devotional bible and would stop in to discuss the bible with me. Even though I started reading my bible often, I could not really understand what I was reading. Even a simple sentence seemed confusing to me. It was weird how I could not understand a simple passage in the bible yet had no problem writing complex university papers.

Time passed and I started talking to Daniel and his family again quite a bit. He was about to graduate from university and I was contemplating going out to his grad. I missed him now more than ever. His dad would try to comfort me and guide me, but he wasn't sure what the right thing to do was either. Daniel's dad knew how much I still loved him. Daniel told me our prom picture was still in his dad's living room, even though we hadn't been together for years. He hadn't replaced my picture with Daniel's girlfriend's picture either. I wondered if Daniel's dad hoped, as I had, we would get back together. In the end though, I decided not to go to his graduation.

It was my last year of university. I graduated with my education degree and figured since Marc had left me, there was nothing holding me back from moving to Thunder Bay. I applied for a couple of teaching jobs and was waiting for an interview. Then one afternoon, about two months after Marc and I had broken up, my heart started aching for him. Tears flowed for a long time that afternoon. I realized I was in love with two men and neither of them wanted me. What was wrong with me? I took out a piece of paper and made a list comparing the two men. Both had one older brother about two years older and no other siblings. Both were French. Both came form broken homes. Both made me laugh. My daughter loved both of them. Both of them left me without warning. Both had broken my heart. Both had given me a red rose and a teddy bear. Then the differences: Marc truly gave me a single red rose. My unlisted phone number was Marc's old number. Marc left me only two months ago. I lived in the same city as Marc. I had loved Daniel for five years and was somehow keeping the vow to him of everlasting love. Both were good-looking. Daniel wanted to be a cop, Marc a teacher. Then in the middle of crying through my lists I realized if they both showed up at my door at the same time I would not be able to decide between the two. This made me cry even harder. In my desperation, I cried out to Jesus. I made a pledge to Him: I would let Him chose for me. I told Jesus my three options…Daniel, Marc, or no one. My pledge to Jesus was that I would do nothing at all. I told him whichever one got a hold of me first or I saw first would be the one I was to be with. If neither of them did, then I would know I was to be with neither of them. Jesus could pick my husband. I also confessed I was going to quit looking because I always messed it up, and I was not the only one getting hurt. My daughter's heart was being broken in the process. Eventually, I cried myself to sleep.

A day or two later the muscles in my shoulder started to twitch and my neck was really sore. The muscles on one side had spasmed so badly, my arm had twisted up and was stuck to my chest and my shoulder was stuck to my head. It was very painful and I didn't know what to do. When I would get hospitalized, Marc would watch my daughter and before him Sarah would watch her. It was September, but all of my friends graduated in the summer, Sarah now lived in another province and Marc was no longer a part of my life. I decided to call the people in my church to see if there was someone who could watch my daughter. Thankfully, another single parent offered to help.

At the hospital, the doctors were very concerned and had talked about sending me by medi-vac to Winnipeg. I was scared and no longer really knew anyone in the city. It didn't take me long before I decided to call Marc even though I didn't know what to say. It had been months since we last spoke. The phone started ringing and to my surprise Marc answered the phone. I told him I was about to have a spinal tap and I was scared. He came down to the hospital an hour or so later. Marc looked amazing and smelled sooo good. I on the other hand looked like a truck just hit me. When it was time for him to leave, I didn't want him to go. Marc gave me a long hug goodbye and then left. In that moment, I knew I didn't want to spend another day without him in my life. The doctors never figured out what was wrong with me and after a couple of days I was better.

In hopes that Marc and I would get back together, I had decided to take another two degrees in education. It would take about two years to complete the degrees, which was what Marc had left to finish his degree. School was about to start and I was hoping I would run into Marc in the hallways at school.

It was not too long after my stint at the hospital Marc and I got back together. We resolved no one was going to know we were dating again. He didn't tell his roommates or family and I didn't tell my daughter or family. This went on for close to two months. Marc would come over late at night long after my daughter had gone to bed. We would spend time talking in each other's arms. We had both agreed my daughter would not find out unless we were staying together permanently. I told Marc she wouldn't be able to handle losing him twice.

Then one night, Marc and I fell asleep on my sectional couch. Marc was on one side and I was on the other. We woke in the morning when my daughter came into the living room. She grabbed Marc's face and looked at him intently. She leaned into him and whispered, "I love you Marc." Marc gave her a big hug and told her he loved her too. I of course started crying. Marc looked at me and I knew we were going to be a family.

As time passed Marc quickly discovered my daughter and I were both plagued with night terrors. There were many nights she and I awoke in fear. The night terrors weren't nearly as bad when Marc stayed the night. One of the nights Marc didn't stay at my place, I dreamt I was at a fairground. It was dawn and no one was at the fair yet. I went in and could hear the sound of a Jack-In-The-Box playing in the background- doo doo doodle doo doo doot doot…I paid to get in to the fair and then was taken into an office in an upper room. There sitting in the middle of the room on a chair was a priest. A demon was ripping out the priest's intestines when I noticed satan standing there watching. I started screaming, but there was no way out. He looked at me and told me he would give me one chance to call for help so I had better choose wisely. I thought for a moment and then started yelling for my oldest brother. Satan started laughing at me and I woke up screaming. As I opened my eyes I looked at my door and I thought for sure I could see satan leaning on my doorpost still laughing at me. I rubbed my eyes and the image was gone. I ran for my bible and hugged it tightly as I slept. How I wished Marc was there to curl into and to keep me safe.

Father's day rolled around and my daughter again asked Marc if he would be her dad. This time he said yes. She started calling him dad right away. A month had passed and I found out I was pregnant. Neither of us was sure how to respond. After a long walk, we decided to keep the baby. At three months pregnant, we told our families. They were all happy for us. Marc's mom jumped on him when we told her I was expecting.

We moved in together that fall with plans to move to Thompson to have our baby. We finished our course work in February and moved to Thompson.

Two days before we were to move I was driving to the grocery store when I was rear-ended. My stomach hit the steering wheel and I went into labor. It was too soon to have the baby and the doctors did everything they could to stop the labor. By God's grace, my labor finally stopped, my baby was going to be fine so the doctors discharged me.

We moved to Thompson and about six weeks later, on April 9, 2001, I gave birth to a beautiful baby girl. Marc and I cried when I delivered her. She was so perfect. We now had two daughters and a family to call our own. We settled down, found a church to attend, and Marc was soon offered a job just out of town. Life was good. I was growing up and I believed my past was finally behind me.

Lo, children are the inheritance of Jehovah; the fruit of the womb is a reward.
~Psalm 127:3~

I Do

Under three things the earth quakes, and under four it is not able to bear up: for a servant when he reigns; and a fool when he is filled with food; for a hateful woman when she is married; Proverbs 30:21-23 MKJV

I was at home one afternoon when Marc came in with a bouquet of beautiful long stemmed roses. He walked into the living room with them, got down on one knee and proposed. I threw my arms around his neck and said yes. We started making wedding plans almost immediately.

Thoughts about my past constantly plagued me knowing I had not told Marc everything about me. I had lied to him about the abortions. The first abortion I blamed solely on the medication and did not acknowledge I still had a choice and I told him the same lie I told everyone else; the second baby died as a result of a miscarriage and left the abortion completely out of the story.

I believed I did not deserve to have him as a husband, so I did almost everything I could to make him leave me. I would throw his wedding band at him and tell him I wanted nothing to do with him. At other times I would have unrealistic expectations of him and if he stumbled, I made sure he knew about it. This included bringing up every wrong thing he had ever done to me. Everything was a lose-lose situation. I really wanted to be married to Marc, but I wanted him to be somebody he wasn't and I continually pretended I was somebody I could not be.

After much trial and tribulation Marc and I were finally married. We were wed in a quaint chapel in a tiny little museum town just outside of Brandon. We did it! We were married and we could now have a fresh start at our new life.

A few weeks after getting married, I took a pregnancy test and sure enough I was pregnant again. Excitement and fear overwhelmed me. I wasn't sure how Marc was going to react. Neither of us had a job and the summer was just about to begin. We had some money from the wedding which was to tie us over until the fall, but there were no job prospects in sight.

Shortly after taking the pregnancy test Marc came home. I asked him to come outside with me and told him I was pregnant. He wasn't sure how to react to the news. I just cried. He asked me what we were going to do. I told him God had always provided for me and I trusted Him to come through for us. Marc wasn't so sure, but he didn't fight me on it. We decided we were not going to tell anyone about the baby until Marc got a job.

A week later, Marc got a call from the principal in his home town. She told him a position had opened up and asked him if he would like it. He told her he would take the job. We were very excited to get out of Thompson and move to his home town. God had provided and I was grateful. We gave the news to everyone we were not only moving, but we were also expecting a baby.

Three weeks later we moved to Marc's home town where his dad was still living. As we were driving, the sky became dark and a storm was starting to brew. The weather was bizarre. I had never seen the sky in such a shade of cloudy green before. As we approached the village, a massive rainbow appeared. The rainbow stretched from one side of the road the other. To enter the town we had to drive through the middle of the rainbow. As we were approaching the rainbow all I could do was think about the story I had heard about Noah and the flood. The rainbow stood for God's promise to never again flood the entire earth. I wondered if this rainbow was a promise our lives would never be the same again, we were finally going to have peace and my past was finally going to be left behind.

Then I saw another powerful angel come down from heaven. He was dressed in a cloud, and there was a rainbow over his head. His face was like the sun, and his legs were like columns of fire.
~Revelations 10:1~

The Walls Begin to Crumble

They go around her on her walls by day and night; and evil and sorrow are in her midst. Psalm 55:10 MKJV

Some say time heals all wounds. I say time allows them to fester and take root. It didn't seem to matter how hard I tried to forget my past or how good I tried to be or how much I tried to change, my past always eventually came back to haunt me- in one way or another…

At about five months pregnant I realized there was something seriously wrong with me. I was having trouble breathing and felt very nauseous. At first I thought I had the flu, but the pain in my stomach began to increase. Marc took me to the hospital in the next town over. With in no time, Marc rushed me off to Yorkton which was an hour away.

Upon arrival at the Yorkton hospital, the specialist gave us the grim news. The doctor wasn't sure what was wrong exactly, but he thought it might be my appendix. Marc and I needed to decide what we wanted to do. If it was my appendix I needed surgery, which meant there was a risk to both our son and I whether I go the surgery or not. If it wasn't my appendix and I got the surgery, there was a risk of my son not surviving the surgery. Either way there was a risk to our son. Oh how I cried. What were we going to do? Could I live with myself if my son died in my womb? I wasn't too sure. With time ticking away, we finally decided the surgery was our best option. If God was real, I hoped He would let my son live. It was so terrifying thinking about the possibility of losing my only son, but it seemed to be a life and death decision- I was hoping for life.

The surgeon discovered the problem was with my appendix. He told us there was a lot of puss in my stomach, but the surgery went well. I was to remain calm and get plenty of bed rest so I would not lose the baby. Thoughts of worry filled my every waking thought. It was so difficult staying calm then fear overwhelmed me and I started crying. There seemed to be a million thoughts roaming through my head when exhaustion kicked in and I eventually fell asleep. I thanked God when we were given the word my son and I were both going to live. Relief hardly begins to describe the emotion that swept over me. A few days later I was discharged and sent home to finish recuperating.

Two months later Christmas rolled around. My family came down for Christmas and I was so happy. It was a wonderful Christmas. Marc and I had all of our parents together for the first time since our wedding. We had a great feast with much music and singing. I loved having not only all our parents, but quite a few of my siblings as well. The holidays came to an end and so did my joy. Creeping around the corner was destruction no one ever saw coming. There was a dark side of my husband that was about to be exposed.

One day while Marc was at work, shortly after turning on the computer in our living room, disturbing images started flashing all over the computer. Irritation was instant. Immediately thoughts of one of my brothers sitting looking at pornography while at my house flashed through my head. It really upset me because they all knew how I felt about that whole industry. I remembered Jesus had said anyone who looks at a woman lustfully has already committed adultery with her in his heart; I believed what was written was true. Not to mention the fact that I figured if you didn't want your daughter, mother, sister, auntie or grandmother in porn then you shouldn't be looking at it because those women were someone else's daughters, mothers, sisters, aunts or grandmothers. Nothing good ever comes from pornography and I wanted nothing to do with it in my house or life.

When I talked to Marc about it he seemed weird. He said all of the right things but his body language spoke something very different. I couldn't quite put my finger on it, but something seemed off. The next day I looked into the history and instantly knew it was not my brothers. The date the porn sites were visited was on December 23; two days before my family arrived. The man I loved and trusted was the one who betrayed me. I was totally distraught. What was I to think or do. A rage built up in me like I had not felt in years. It was a very long couple of hours waiting for Marc to get home. There was plenty of time for the rage to increase to the point that it took a hold of me.

Eventually, my husband walked in the door and I sent my girls out to play. Then the show down began. Marc bold faced denied looking at porn. Computers don't lie and I knew the only person in the house who could have been on the computer was him. After much screaming and yelling he finally admitted the he had gone on while we girls were in bed sleeping. Feelings of the horrendous violation I faced as a child filled me all over again. I remembered how my father had sexually abused me at night while I was sleeping. Knowing my husband was looking at sexual images while I slept enraged me to such a degree I was afraid of what I wanted to do to him.

There was something familiar about his reaction to being caught. It reminded me of my father's reaction. He seemed sorry he was caught. Not sorry about what he had done though. Marc had to go! There was no way I could let him stay at home even a moment longer. He packed his bags and went to live with his dad.

Word spread around town pretty quick my husband and I had split up. I was totally distraught and miserable without him. I told my mom I wanted a divorce and asked her if she would help me. She asked if I was sure I wanted a divorce and when I told her I was, to my relief, she agreed to help me.

A few weeks later reality sunk in. I started thinking about Daniel and thought he never would have done this to me. Somehow I rationalized a man who wanted nothing to do with me would never have hurt me like this. Everything felt hopeless and completely overwhelming. Bitter tears swept across my cheeks. My chest heaved with each sob as air tried to fill my lungs. I could hardly breathe. With each tear that fell not only did my heart painstakingly ache, but my stomach started to ache as well. I had cried myself into labor, but I was only seven months pregnant. It was too soon to have the baby. With no one to drive me, there was no choice but to call my husband. He and his dad came down to the house right away. A smug smile filled my face when Marc noticed I was no longer wearing my wedding rings. I knew seeing the rings on the shelf hurt him and I was glad. I wanted him to hurt as much as I was. I wanted my pound of flesh.

Marc's dad watched the girls while my husband drove me to the hospital in Yorkton an hour and a half away. To say the ride was quiet for the first while would be a gross understatement; you could cut the silence with a knife. We tried making light conversation about what name we were going to give our son. There was such a mixed batch of emotions running through my veins. On the one hand, I couldn't stop thinking about our unborn son and on the other hand I couldn't stop thinking about my feelings for my husband. I hated him and missed him all at the same time. Sure, I was relieved he was taking me to the hospital, but I didn't want him to know he was the only one I wanted to have with me in that moment. I didn't want him to know I still loved him and wanted him back home. I didn't want him to know losing him was tearing me apart. I wanted him to think I was fine on my own without him. I wanted him to think I was happier with him not in my life, and our daughters were better off without him. The truth was us three girls needed him and missed him terribly.

When we got to the hospital the doctor asked me what happened. What was I to say? So, I told him there was a family crisis which upset me and I started crying. Thankfully, the doctor was able to stop the labor. He kept me in the hospital for a few days under observation. Late night phone calls with Marc began a line of communication. We eventually came to terms and I agreed to let him move back home. He told me he was going to stop looking at pornography and I desperately wanted to believe him.

A month later, we welcomed out premature son into the world. Our son seemed to be born healthy and normal, but a few hours later all of his vital signs began dropping. The doctors were contemplating medevaccing our son to the nearest neonatal center. The whole thing was both frightening and depressing. Only one person come to see my son in the hospital and my husband left a few hours after our son was born. Marc couldn't handle seeing our son in such a state, so he decided he would go home where he thought he could be useful. Instead of my son spending the first 24 hours of his life in my arms, he spent it in an incubator full of tubes and wires. He should have been in my arms where I could rock him and love him. How I longed to hold my child. In my eyes, he was going to redeem the male race and I couldn't even hold him. After about twenty-four hours, our son was out of the danger zone and I was finally able to hold him.

There was overwhelming joy when I got to hold my son for the first time. I loved this little boy more than words could ever begin to describe. This boy was going to love me and I knew it. His love for me was going to be uncorrupted and I couldn't wait to embrace him. The love that permeated through my son into me overwhelmed me. It felt so incredibly good to be loved by him even though he was only two days old. There are no words to describe the pure love I felt for my newly born son.

After all of the complications with my son and my Marc's addiction, I foolishly decided I never wanted to have another child with him again. So, I convinced Marc to have a vasectomy and a few weeks later he had the procedure. Time passed and life had gone back to normal. Then one day I had opened the cable bill and noticed there was an extra $2.00 charge on the account. When I saw what the charge was for I was enraged; it was for pornography advertising. Immediately I called the cable company and asked them why this charge was on my bill. They told me we had ordered it. I asked the gentlemen on the other end of the phone if there was any possible way a mistake had been made. He told me no. After explaining my marriage hinged on his answer he sadly affirmed what I already knew. The only way to get that charge was to order the channel. I was furious! I was in a total state of disbelief and wasn't even sure how to approach the subject. What was I going to do? Hate still permeated my body from the first go of this. After approaching Marc with the bill, he said he had no idea what I was talking about and denied the whole thing. Not only was he a good actor, but I also didn't want it to be true so I decided to accept his lie and dropped the issue.

We decided we needed to get away. We went on a three week vacation out to Quebec. It was a blessing to get away from home. There were some tense moments on the trip, but overall it was good for us to get away. At the end of July we came home where we spent the rest of the summer.

August was very hot. My son started to have petite mal seizures in high volumes. Terror gripped my heart. This was the third major health problem that had the potential of stealing my son's life. One afternoon, I held my seven month old son in my arms just rocking him back and forth. I called out to the God of heaven and earth begging for Him to give me my son's seizures. My son had not even committed any sin and he did not deserve to have these seizures I pleaded. However, I confessed to God I had sinned plenty in my life and I did deserve it. Through swollen tear filled eyes, I cried and cried as I begged God to remove the seizures from my son and to give them to me. Slowly I cried myself to sleep.

The next morning I woke and went to have breakfast, but before I went to eat, I decided to go to the bathroom. All of a sudden my side started to hurt. The pain began to increase to a level I had never felt before in my life. Panic stricken shrieks for Marc echoed throughout the house. He came running into the washroom where he found me with my head hanging in the toilet vomiting uncontrollably. I could not believe how much I had thrown up. My husband called the ambulance and a friend down the street came to watch the kids. The pain seemed to last for an eternity. Approximately 45 minutes later, the ambulance arrived. As soon as the paramedics opened the door, I stopped throwing up. They placed me on the gurney and rushed me to the hospital. By the time we arrived at the hospital I felt fine as if nothing had happened. There was blood in my urine so the doctors thought I had passed a kidney stone, however, the ultrasound found no evidence of there being any stones whatsoever. We just chalked it up to another one of my weird sicknesses.

A couple of weeks later, my son went for his brain scan. We were relieved and confused to learn there was no evidence of seizures in my son's brain. He also never had another seizure again. God had answered my prayer. The seizures were not the only problem our son had. He had a tear duct that had not opened and he needed surgery on his eye. The doctors told us if it didn't open on its own by the age of two, then they would need to operate on it.

Over the course of the next year I often stared out our kitchen window at the huge hill on the other side of the street. I slowly started getting the urge to climb what seemed like a mountain to me. This urge was particularly strange because this hill frightened me something awful. There were snakes, coyotes and wild dogs out there. The last thing I wanted to do was go anywhere near that hill. Months passed and the urge got stronger and stronger. I said to my husband one day, that as crazy as it seemed, I felt like God wanted me to climb that hill. He agreed- I sounded crazy.

Our son was scheduled for surgery on his eye to open the tear duct a around his second birthday. I was extremely nervous about the surgery and did not want him to have it, but knew the tear duct needed to open. The night before we were to take him for his surgery was freezing cold outside. The temperature was around -40°C with no wind. Of course, this was the night the urge to climb the hill was so overwhelming I went and told Marc I needed to climb that hill right now. Even though I was pretty sure he thought I had completely lost it, he nonchalantly told me to do whatever I thought I needed to do.

After feeding my son, I cleaned his goopy eye and got dressed for the weather. Terror began gripping the very fiber of my being. What was I thinking? I kept picturing this big black dog chasing me down and attacking me, yet I still felt I needed to conquer *the mountain*. I kissed my husband and set out on my quest. It was dark and ominous outside. A haze had filled the streets and not a sound could be heard. Everything was still.

My heart was pounding a million miles per minute wondering when the dog was going to come out and attack me. After arriving safely at the bottom of the hill, I looked what seemed to be way up. I could hardly see the top of the hill through the fog. Determined after making it this far, I had best start climbing. The snow was incredibly deep. I had to start crawling on my knees because the snow came up to my waist creating great difficulties for me. Finally, I reached the top and looked out over the town. The sight was amazing. The haze covered the whole valley but when I looked up the night's sky was crystal clear and beautiful. The stars were so bright. I lifted my hands up and in frustration and fear I shouted to God, "I am here now what?" It was only about 10 seconds before panic gripped me. The panic was so terrorizing it was as if someone had taken a hold of the front of my coat and shook fear down to my roots. I started running down the hill when I fell causing me to tumble the rest of the way down. Jumping to my feet and without stopping, I ran all the way home. When I got in the door I could hardly breathe. The cold night's air burnt the back of my throat and lungs. Not being able to figure out for the life of me why I did what I just did, I was relieved it was over.

The next day we took our son to the city for his surgery. When we arrived at the hospital I told my husband I wasn't sure if he still needed the surgery. Our son's eye was clear for the first time in two years. The doctor took a look at his eye and told us the tear duct had opened. Wow! This was the second time we no longer had to deal with a medical problem. This was very exciting news.

A few months had passed and the comforts of home were rattled once again. I took my three children north to visit my family back in Thompson even though Marc couldn't come. We were gone for about five days and had a wonderful time even though secretly I worried about my husband, but there was nothing I could do. It was about a ten hour drive back home and I left my parents place later than I should have. We arrived home late where we were greeted at the door by Marc who was acting very strange. I was exhausted getting off the road, but Marc wanted to be intimate. However, I knew there was something terribly wrong with him, but could not figure out what it was. A little of afraid and not sure what to do, I lied to him and said I was too tired and pretended to fall asleep. The dark eeriness of our room completely enveloped me and so I did what I always did to cope…I fell into an incredibly deep sleep.

The next day, as soon as my husband left for work, I went to see what he had been doing on the computer while I was gone. Just as I had suspected, he had done it again. There was pornography all over the computer. I packed up all of my husband's things into garbage bags and waited for him to come home. It was over! All I could hear in my head was, "He almost cost our son his life and that didn't even make him stop". I thought of all the words I wanted to say to hurt him with. Now I knew Marc had a sexual addiction and I believed it was going to ruin our family.

When Marc got home I told him he had one chance to tell me the truth. He did not take that chance. I told him I knew about the computer and he had not stopped looking at pornography. He again denied it at first but eventually admitted it. The worst part wasn't even the fact he was looking at porn; it was the lying and secrecy. It seemed so dark and dirty. He moved back to his dad's that afternoon and I was alone again.

Time passed and I still wanted the divorce. I told him it was important he still maintain a relationship with his children though. However, if he tried fighting the custody or the divorce I would ruin his life- it was his choice whether it was going to be a messy divorce or not. The whole time all I wanted was for him to get on his knees and beg me to forgive him and I would. If he cried and plead with me not to leave him I would forgive him right there in that moment. He never did though.

A week after he moved in with his dad, we started talking late in the evening after the kids went to bed. I wanted to believe somehow there was still a chance this marriage could be saved. Just as the time before, I started leaning on God for strength. I prayed constantly about the situation and begged God to fix it. Slowly my heart began softening towards Marc. Then over time, Marc and I agreed to give it one more chance and I let him move back home.

It was incredibly difficult living; it seemed hard to just breathe. It wasn't long before I sought professional help. I was headed for a mental breakdown and I knew it. The lies began to drive me insane. Deciphering what to believe about anyone or anything became impossible. Then the delusions started. There were times I would look at my hands and I knew they we mine but I didn't recognize them. Or I would look at my hands and some days they would look really big and then other days they would look so tiny. I knew I was in serious trouble. My counselor scheduled a psych evaluation and to my pleasant surprise, the psychiatrist agreed with my point of view regarding pornography. He told me that because of the identity crisis in my marriage, I was having delusions that had to do with my identity as a result of extreme stress. With this new information I approached my husband and asked him if he would be willing to go to marriage counseling. To my relief, my husband agreed to see a counselor.

After the first visit we knew the counseling was not going to be a whole lot of help to us. The counselor did not see a problem with pornography. Feelings of isolation, rejection as a wife, bitterness, anger and resentment often overwhelmed me. I was angry at my husband; I was angry at myself and I was angry at God. It seemed so unfair I was raised with sexual abuse and then was given a husband who had a sexual addiction. I would cry out to God why, what had I done to deserve this life. I hated my life and just wanted to die. The only thing that stopped me from actually taking my life was the fear of what would happen to my three children if I wasn't around.

I started thinking about all of the things my biological father had done. Watching my husband go through a sexual addiction, I realized my dad probably couldn't control himself either. If my husband could risk the life of his child and not see a problem then what happened to my father was far worse. This moved me to compassion and forgiveness. It is hard to fathom the tortures that must have been going through my biological father's mind before he gave in to temptation. Then one night I sat down and wrote my biological father a letter. I told him I forgave him for what he did to me, but I didn't want him to contact me. I then sealed the envelope and mailed it to his mother's address. Whether he received the letter or not I may never know, but hoped he had.

…forgive us our sins, as we have forgiven those who have sinned against us. Matthew 6:9 ISV

On top of my extremely stressful home life, I started having severe cramping every month with my periods. The pain was excruciating. The doctor gave me injections to relieve the pain. However, eventually the doctor sent me to see a specialist. I was scheduled for exploratory surgery a few weeks later. The results came back I had endometriosis, which is a disease with no cure. Basically what happens is the lining of the uterus a woman sheds every month is supposed to leave the body. For whatever reason, parts of my lining were no longer only in the uterus. Pieces of the lining were growing on the outside of my organs and had no way of leaving the body. So every month this would occur and I would be doubled over with pain.

Between our broken marriage and traveling every month for medical assistance, we knew we needed a change; if we did not move our marriage was not going to last. At the end of the school year, my husband was offered a job in Silver Lake and we took it. Marc promised me he was going to leave his addiction behind and we were going to have a fresh start in our marriage. I hoped with all my heart this was true.

*It is better not to take an oath than
to take an oath and not keep it.
~Ecclesiastes 5:5~ BBE*

On The Edge

They are rebuilding the rebellious and the evil city and are completing its walls, and have joined the foundations. Ezra 4:12

Moving to a new town and a new home, gave me new hope and a new passion for my husband. We got our new home set up and the kids registered for school. Everything was going really well. It had been close to a year since my husband and I had been back together. We weren't fighting as much and the kids seemed happy to be in a new place as well. For the first time in a few years, I enjoyed intimacy with my husband. It seemed like our marriage was where it should be and I was starting to trust him again.

One night I fell asleep early. As I slept I heard an alarming warning in my dream. I didn't see anyone in my dream, but I heard these chilling words, "Get up! The devil is in your house!" I awoke with such a fright and immediately started praying. For whatever reason, I knew without even getting up, my husband had been looking at pornography on the computer.

I headed straight for the computer where my fears were confirmed; the addiction was still there. I did notice something different this time though, there was very little pornography viewed. There was only a few minutes worth, rather than hours. Even though it was not yet morning, I woke my husband up out of a deep sleep to confront him. This was the quickest he had ever admitted what he had done. I let him go back to sleep but we talked about it later. The evening came and after the children went to bed we sat down to talk. Marc said he couldn't help himself and that he wasn't even looking for it. He said after a few minutes he got off and wasn't sure why he was even on it. I somehow strangely believed him. We talked for a good chunk of the night. I wanted his addiction to be gone and yet it wasn't. What I was going to do? I had no one to talk to about it and I was confused.

Marc knew I was hurting and needed someone to talk to. He told me I could talk to his mom about it and so I did. She was amazing to talk with and I felt incredibly blessed to have her in my life. We talked for hours and she helped me work through what I was going to do. I was hurt, angry and confused, but I wanted to fight. I began to realize there was more to the situation than what met the eye.

Marc and I had a long talk on the porch and he said he wanted to change but didn't know what to do. We made a pact we were going to fight for our marriage and together we could beat this thing. I ordered a book called, "Every Man's Battle" and read it. The book was helpful to me. It seemed like we were going to be able to beat this thing after all. I believed Marc had finally won his battle.

We soon started talking about having another child. Not only did I want another child, but I also believed this baby would help change our marriage. The thought of the horrible memories of being pregnant with our son plagued me. I didn't want the memories of my last pregnancy to be so depressing. We talked about getting Marc's vasectomy reversed for a very long time. The cost for the procedure was very expensive and we could not afford it. Even though we stopped talking about having another baby, my heart still yearned for another child.

We began meeting people in Silver Lake. With each person we met, our inhibitions decreased. We started partying every weekend and drinking on a regular basis. It was not long before we started not only drinking in front of our children, but we also started partying at home. We were often inebriated and I would have a glass or two of wine almost every day, sometimes even before lunch. I became more and more flirtatious and enjoyed the attention I received.

That summer was hot! We spent most of our time out at the local beach where most of the women wore bikinis. Fear set in because I wanted my husband to focus on me and not the other women. Even though I had three children, I was in great shape and decided I would flaunt it in hopes Marc's focus would remain on me. That week I went and bought a lot of bathing suits, all of which were very revealing. I wore short shorts and bikinis all summer. My husband told me I was the "eye candy" at the beach. I blushed, but secretly I knew he was right and I lavished in the power which came with this. I was keeping Marc's attention and the attention of every other man there.

Summer was coming to an end and there were problems with the house we were renting, so we decided it was time move and possibly buy a house of our own. We looked at the housing available in our little town, but there was nothing. My parents had moved to a town twenty minutes away and after much friendly persistence from my parent's carpenter, we decided to look at housing in the town they were living in.

A couple of weeks later, we were happy home owners. We were going to get a fresh start and our past, including the hopelessness, stress, and abuse, were all going to be behind us. Only my parents knew us, so we could be whoever we wanted to be. I was looking forward to that more than anything else.

We took possession of the house on September the first. With this new start we decided we were going to try and have another child. Marc was going to go for the surgery to get his vasectomy reversed. We had an extra room built into the floor plans in hopes we would soon have a new addition to our family. Life had pleasantly switched on us. We went from seemingly hopeless and living in complete wickedness to a very promising life. A fresh start was exactly what I needed.

For there is hope of a tree, if it be cut down, that it will sprout again, and that the tender branch thereof will not cease.
~Job 14:7~ KJV

Hope Restored-Faith Renewed

Who without reason for hope, in faith went on hoping, so that he became the father of a number of nations, as it had been said, "So will your seed be." Romans 4:18 BBE

YHWH (Yahweh), I AM WHO I AM, was soon going to be the center of my thinking. I began searching for God and as I drew closer to Him, He in turn drew closer to me...

My parent's carpenter was now not only our carpenter, but our friend as well. We confided in him about our plans for another child and he faithfully kept it a secret. Approximately six weeks had passed when Marc and I came to the heartbreaking decision we could not afford the cost of the procedure. With a heavy heart I tried to put the thought of having another child behind me. I was completely heartbroken and yet secretly I did not want to give up hope that somehow, someday I would carry another child in my womb.

The carpenter would drop by almost every Sunday morning to see if we were going to church. Our answer was always no, but we filtered the no with a ton of excuses. Finally, a few months later, we decided to attend a service at our friend's church. The people were very warm and inviting. We were hooked and loved our Sunday mornings. I had never felt so loved and accepted by a group or community before.

After attending the church for only a couple of weeks, I was invited to the ladies' retreat but could not afford to go. I wasn't sure if I even really wanted to go. I didn't really know anyone and I had never been away from my family before for more than a few hours at a time. However, this one lady in the church kept asking me to come wondering what it would take to get me to go. Finally, knocking my pride and stubbornness down a peg or two, I told her I could not afford to go. I thought she would stop asking me, but instead she said the church could sponsor me to go. I was flabbergasted. Why was she being so kind to me? I didn't even know her. Without even asking my husband, I agreed to go on the retreat.

The Christmas season seeped in. One cold winter's night, I had a strange dream. In my dream there was an angel who came to tell me I was going to give birth. Later I asked God what I was to call the child; He told me Rauel. Then I asked, "What will the child's middle name be?" And God told me Malachi. When I woke up I thought the dream wasn't just a dream. With great excitement and nervousness, I told my husband about the dream. He told me I was not a bible character and to let it go. I was so hurt he was not willing to even talk about it with me and foolishly I thought he would at least toy with notion, but he was angry instead.

Something was stirring in me. My thinking was beginning to change. Not that I could describe what was happening, but I began to see my life a little different than I used to. One night I asked God to help me quit smoking. I realized it was grieving Him, but I could only quit if He helped me. Also, I wanted to quite just in case there was a chance I was going to be pregnant. A few days later I quit smoking with only a little discomfort. Marc quit at the same time, which made it easier for me.

Christmas had passed and my period was late. My period was never late. A couple of days later I went to the doctor for a pregnancy test but it came back negative. Eight days later I went back again and it was still negative. I was confused. Was my dream real? I was starting to think it was real, but then why were the tests negative? On the ninth day I was disappointed when my period started. Did I just want a baby so bad that my body was fooled into thinking I was pregnant?

A week or two later, it was time for the ladies' retreat. I got all packed up and headed to Winkler for the retreat. Within the first ten minutes of listening to the guest speaker I was furious. I felt like an idiot and completely trapped. Not only was I fuming, but I didn't want anyone to know how angry I was. I was angry at God and at the situation in total. I felt like I had been tricked into going. Had I known what the speaker was going to talk about I never would have gone. She started talking about the pains of sexual abuse and the need to forgive. The last thing I wanted to talk or think about was my abuse. How dare she dig up my past without warning? I was completely blindsided by her and did not appreciate it. Who did she think she was? She made me remember the torments of what my father had done to me in front of all of these people! I went back to my room after her speech and pulled out the bottle of wine I had brought and the huge container of chocolate. I figured between the alcohol and chocolate, I would be able to relax.

The woman who invited me to go to the retreat wound up being my roommate. She stayed up talking with me, until the wee hours of the morning. I could not believe the wisdom this woman had. She told me about spiritual things I had only felt, but she talked about them as if they were fact and she could prove it. I was amazed and wanted to learn more. Morning quickly encroached and so with little sleep, we attended the next session.

No longer angry about the night before, I came ready to learn. I learned the definition I had made up in my head regarding what a godly woman looked like was completely and totally unrealistic to attain on my own. This godly woman was completely perfect and I was striving to be her in my own strength.

I can do all things through Christ who strengthens me. Philippians 4:13 MKJV

That night something happened I never expected. The speaker asked us to think about all of the women we needed to forgive and to write down their names on a piece of paper. She instructed if we were willing, we were to then put the paper in the basket to symbolize the act of forgiving. I just sat there dumbfounded at first. Then I started doing something I had not done in a long time. I cried.

There was something in the room with us that took my breath away. I did not know a whole lot about the Spirit of God, only what little I had heard in Church. I suspected what overtook my mind, body and emotions was the Holy Spirit. The tears started flooding from my eyes. There were only a few women on my list but with each person I chose to forgive, the harder I cried. I started crying so hard my nose started bleeding. I took off to the washroom and just sobbed. I had not cried like that since I was pregnant with my son. It was very freeing and confusing at the same time. Why was I crying? I didn't normally cry like this. A group of women came into the washroom to comfort me and I was very grateful. The tears continued on and off for the rest of the weekend.

That night I stayed up late talking with my roommate. The next day the retreat ended. It was a long drive home. I dropped off my roommate at her house which was in one of the neighboring towns. She had said over the weekend she felt like I was Rauel Malachi. Could this be true? How was that even possible? Those words filtered through my mind as I drove home. As I was driving, I came to the top of a beautiful valley. It was as if the sun had kissed the tops of the trees. I pulled my car over and just cried. Rauel means friend of God and Malachi means God's messenger. As the sun was beaming in the car, I looked towards heaven and with tear-filled eyes; I said if it was true, if the name was actually for me, then I accepted it. The sun's warmth brushed my cheeks and I felt complete awe for my Creator. I wept tears of joy and confusion on and off the rest of the way home. When I got back to town I stopped at the church not quite ready to go home yet. The sanctuary was quiet while I prayed. I thanked God for the changes He had made in me and for the peace that had come over me. At home I told my husband about the whole thing. I felt so different; there was a peace I had never felt before in my entire life. It was strange and yet I hoped this feeling would last forever.

After the retreat, I was invited to take a bible study and I instantly agreed to attend. The bible study started to shake the foundations I had built up for myself. One of the big kickers for me was I had thought myself to be as close to perfect as one could get. I looked good, I was smart, I always helped others when asked, I believed I was a Christian even though I knew very little about God and never read my bible, I was nice to people, and I was definitely superior to my husband and all of his flaws. However, the bible study called *Down Pour* by James MacDonald started teaching me things I had never considered about myself. We were given an assignment where we had you rate your sin from 1-10. I didn't think I really had any sin, so I had asked the group of ladies I was with to pray God would show me my sin. Not only was I not close to perfection, but I was so littered with sin it was almost unbearable to handle. How could this be? I even had sexual sin when I thought I didn't. I learned the bathing suits I wore were sinfully revealing and being "eye candy" not only grieved God, but also hurt myself, my family, and all those who saw me. It was gut wrenching knowing husbands and wives probably had been affected by what I wore at the beach, church and around the community. It is completely ungodly and sinful to have even a little cleavage because it causes not only men to stumble into adultery, but it torments the wives whose husbands looked at me with lustfulness also. How did I not know this? I thought I looked good like this. It is horrifying to think that while at church men and women where distracted from the word of God because of how I was dressed. My tight pants, low cut shirts and tummy exposure weren't cute, pretty, classy, beautiful or anything else the "world" taught me. It was down right sinful. I was devastated and felt completely naked and exposed.

In the same way, count yourselves dead to sin but alive to God in Christ Jesus. Therefore do not let sin reign in your mortal body so that you obey its evil desires. Do not offer the parts of your body to sin, as instruments of wickedness, but rather offer yourselves to God, as those who have been brought from death to life; and offer the parts of your body to him as instruments of righteousness. For sin shall not

be your master, because you are not under law, but under grace. Romans 6:11-14 NIV

Before starting the bible study I felt pretty self righteous, but now I didn't know what to think. I thought when I did the assignment, there was going to be barely anything and by the time we all got back together the next week, I had booklets full of my sin.

The next part of the assignment was to confess your sin to someone else and ask them to pray for you. I didn't want to tell anyone about all the things I had done. Who could I trust? Finally, I resolved to tell my husband. I figured it would make him feel better about himself after all of the horrible things I had said about how perfect I was and how he was nowhere near close to perfect. The truth of the matter was I was at least equally sinful if not more sinful.

As the study progressed, I slowly began making changes in my life. However, I was trying to change in my own strength and for all the wrong reasons. I loved what appeared to be right and so I wanted to be seen as "right". I did not want to solely change because my sin affected other people; I just wanted to be perfect. Thinking I now knew what was needed to be perfect, I started mimicking those behaviors.

Wild dreams and nightmares began to affect my whole day. I would often dream about Daniel and would wake up feeling totally violated and guilty. Then I would spend the next day or two thinking about him causing the guilt to increase, and yet I couldn't stop no matter how hard I tried. I felt like I was cheating on Marc. However, I would justify to myself that if I knew why Daniel and I broke up ten years ago then I would stop thinking about him. I had myself convinced the not knowing was why I would still think about Daniel all these years later. When we broke up a decade ago I thought by this time I wouldn't even remember his name. Was I ever wrong! Time did not heal that wound and I started believing it never would. The whole situation left me so distraught I decided to confide in a couple in our church. I didn't want Marc to know because I knew it would hurt him. Sheepishly, I made the call and spoke with the wife for quite a while. She and her husband prayed for me and I felt better.

Slowly I began to feel like I was returning to God. I was starting to believe He was real again and I was getting excited. As I began to forgive people for things they had done to me, I noticed I felt better. I was pretty sure I was starting to hear God's voice again too. One afternoon I asked God to show me what had really happened to me with my biological father. In the bible study, I was learning how satan can affect our lives and I knew the devil had to have been involved with what had happened to me.

Lest satan should get an advantage of us: for we are not ignorant of his devices. 2 Corinthians 2:11 KJV

God then showed me how my father was being tormented by demons. The *father of lies* was constantly tempting my father. God showed me how my father tried to resist satan, but after a while my father quit fighting. The day came when my father bought into the lies he was being told, and as a result he started to abuse me. My father, by his own admissions, believed he loved me, but the devil had taught him a very sick and perverted idea of what love was. I began feeling very sorry for my father which led me to forgive him for more of what he had done to me. I started praying God would forgive him too.

The Lord is not slow about his promise, as some people understand slowness, but is being patient with you. He does not want anyone to perish, but wants everyone to come to repentance. 2 Peter 3:9

The revelation of what had happened to my father was earthshaking for me. I had a whole new perspective on what had happened to me. My father didn't really hate me nor did he really think he was hurting me. I now knew it wasn't really my father who wanted to hurt me either. It wasn't really my father who hated me; it was satan the whole time. My father was just a sick little pawn in the devil's scheme, even though he still made the choice, I now knew the truth- satan was behind the whole thing!

And you will know the truth, and the truth will set you free. John 8:32 LITV

Life was changing for my family and I was changing too, but I found life was still very hard. I fought often with my husband and the power struggles were unbearable. I still treated my children poorly and I could not control my temper or my tongue. The most vile, hateful things would come out of my mouth towards my children and my husband. I tried to stop, but I couldn't. There was still a shred of hope that I could truly change once and for all.

Our family started a bible study about Daniel. We were learning what integrity meant for Daniel and what it was going to mean for us as well. That summer we took a trip to British Columbia to visit Marc's family. We took the study along with us on our trip. It was nerve wracking reading my bible in public. I couldn't figure out why I felt so uncomfortable reading God's word around strangers, but I knew I would eventually get used to it.

We had a wonderful three weeks together as a family. Overall, the vacation went well. We came home, however, to a raft of problems. The dryer broke down and so did our well. We had no money left to fix either problem and we weren't sure what we were going to do. I spoke with the woman who was running the bible studies I had been in. She reminded me about a local camp called Christian Enrichment Family Camp she had talked to me about going to. I told her as much as we wanted to go; there was no possible way with everything that had just broken down at home. She told me to have faith that there would be a way for us to go. Really thinking there was no point, I told her I would have faith. A couple of days later the woman called me back and told me our family had just been sponsored to go to camp. I was in complete and total disbelief. I really wanted to go to camp that week and now we could go! Our family packed back up and headed off to camp.

And may the God of hope fill you with all joy and peace in believing, that you may abound in hope through the power of the Holy Spirit.
~Romans 15:13~ MKJV

Return to Righteousness

For we through the Spirit wait for the hope of righteousness out of faith. Galatians 5:5 MKJV

Love covers over a multitude of sin and I am very grateful God sent people along my path to show me the love of Christ. Even though I was sinning and did not recognize my sin, the people God placed in my path knew them. It is a little embarrassing looking back to some of the things I said in my folly, and yet these men and women of God looked passed my foolishness waiting for what God was going to do in me.

We arrived at Christian Enrichment Family Camp and were placed in a cute little cabin beside a fresh-water creek. The sound of the flowing stream could be heard from the open window. The smell of the trees and lake filtered through the cabin and I was filled with gratitude and joy. I was really looking forward to hearing the speakers, even though I had never met them or heard any of their teachings. There was going to be a service every night that week, in a building called the Sheep Shed, and I was looking forward to attending every one of them.

That night we went to our first service. The service was disappointing because I knew whatever the preacher was saying was important, but I could barely understand him. I couldn't figure out why I couldn't understand him though. I have never had a problem understanding people with accents before and was really frustrated. Marc was probably a little annoyed with me constantly asking him what the man was saying. My stomach was also really sore. My belly had swollen so bad I looked like I was about eight months pregnant and I was very uncomfortable.

After the service Ruth, the woman who asked us to attend camp, introduced me to the speakers Jeff and Jane. She had made note of my stomach to the speakers as well, and Jane seamed strangely interested in my predicament. After a few minutes of talking, I joined up with Marc for the night.

It was a little strange being sponsored and so I asked if there was anything my husband and I could do to help out. We were then blessed to help out with the baking that week. I felt much better about being out there and volunteering.

Sadly, I missed the Tuesday night service because my son needed to go to bed early. When the service was over, my daughters joined their brother and I was able to head back towards the Sheep Shed. People were still in the building even though the service had ended. Some were just sitting there and others went up to the front for prayer. I was not very familiar with this way of doing church, but I was not bothered by it either. Marc on the other hand was not comfortable with it at all, and did not see the merit or value in it. As I entered the building my husband left. He didn't care if I stayed, he just didn't want to. All of a sudden I was filled with emotions and I had no idea why. Suddenly I began weeping uncontrollably. I sat down and just cried. Someone brought me some tissue and wrapped a blanket around me. I thought the blanket was weird, but it was comforting.

I finally pulled myself together and left the building. I felt like being alone so I headed towards the lake in hopes my husband wouldn't see me, but to my dismay he had. Marc asked to join me and I said yes. I wanted my husband to share in my experience, but I knew he didn't believe in anything that was happening. However, I wasn't so convinced this wasn't a touch from God. We sat by the lake talking about what had just happened when Marc told me he would never be up at the front in one of those prayer lines. For some reason this hurt me and I no longer wanted to talk about God with him. I was pretty sure God was doing something in me that I had no words for and could not explain to anyone, but I just knew it had to be God. We left the beach and headed off to bed.

I learned a valuable lesson at the service Wednesday night. God's arm is not too short, meaning I made God and what He could do very small in my mind (I am still learning this valuable lesson to this day). That night people were invited to go up to the front for prayers, which I later learned was what people refer to as an alter call. Lo and behold, one of the first people up at the front was Marc. I was in complete awe and shock. Just the night before my husband had said he would never go to the front and the next night here he was up at the front. My heart started pounding and I was incredibly excited. Later I teased him about saying he would never be caught at the front of one of "those" lines. We both still chuckled about it.

As the days began to pass, my stomach was becoming more and more uncomfortable. I felt like I was pregnant. People who knew me were also suspicious of my swollen abdomen. I could feel movement in my stomach and so could others. It was gross, but there was nothing I could do about it.

Thursday afternoon I went down to the beach even though I didn't really feel like swimming. My son was in my arms when I began speaking with Jane. I decided to ask if she would be willing to pray about my son's night terrors. There was no harm in asking for prayer for him, in reality the worst that could happen was nothing. She asked my son about some of his dreams, but he was feeling very shy. I told her about how he was even seeing things at night in his room when he was not quite asleep yet. Jane agreed to get together with my husband and me to pray about the night terrors.

The next morning, the speakers asked Ruth to join Marc and me in the lounge. The lounge is a beautiful room in the main lodge at camp. It has French doors, a fireplace, original Victorian wood casings and some couches. There were a couple of things said just prior to going into the room though that caught my attention. One of the strange things was Jane asking Ruth to bring a notebook to take notes. Even though this was odd, I brushed it off.

> **He who believes and is baptized will be saved, but he who does not believe will be condemned. And miraculous signs will follow to those believing these things: in My name they will cast out demons; they will speak new tongues; they will take up serpents; and if they drink any deadly thing, it will not hurt them. They will lay hands on the sick, and they will be well.** Mark 16:16-18 MKJV

The next five hours changed my entire life...

We went into the room and they closed the door behind us. The warmth of the sun flooded into the room as we sat talking. Then Jeff and Jane started asking me questions about my past and I began to divulge everything. As I talked with them my stomach hurt worse than it had ever before. I even told them about how I always felt like I had a black panther locked up in the pit of my stomach and that it was as if it somehow got loose and would just run rampant in my life. It would then be forced back into its cage and I would lock it up again. Then it would just sit there swinging its tail back and forth waiting for the next time to prowl. As I was telling them this, my stomach began turning and I knew I was going to be sick. Panicked, I told them I had to go because I felt like I was going to throw up. Jane looked at me not the least bit surprised and said, "Yup, here it comes!" I thought to myself, "Here what comes?" Then I threw up a little. My husband was sitting beside me, the speakers were sitting almost in front of us, and Ruth was on another couch taking notes.

> **And when He had called to Him His twelve disciples, He gave them authority over unclean spirits, to cast them out, and to heal all kinds of sickness and all kinds of disease.** Matthew 10:1

Over the next five hours Jesus came and delivered me from the demons that had placed me in bondage. The speakers began calling out demons by their characteristics. In between calling out the demonic, the speakers spoke to me about situations in my past and asked me to either forgive those who hurt me or to repent. I learned to repent means not to just say, "Jesus, I am sorry, please forgive me", but to change your mind or thinking about your sin and to turn from it, it wasn't enough to just say sorry, but my thinking about my sin had to change as well. As my sin was revealed, I would come into agreement with Jesus regarding my sin and confess I had sinned, repent and seek forgiveness. I needed to remove the unforgiveness in my heart as well because it is written, **"For if you forgive men their trespasses, your heavenly Father will also forgive you; but if you do not forgive men their trespasses, neither will your Father forgive your trespasses.**" (Matthew 6:14,15 BBE) Forgiving others was key for my deliverance. If I wanted to be forgiven by Christ then I needed to forgive. If I had chosen to hold onto my unforgiveness, which I had every "right" to hold on to, I would never have been set free. Just because I had the right to my emotions and beliefs, didn't make either of them good. My hatred for those who had hurt me caused me more suffering then I could ever have imagined. Because I was not willing to forgive, I would often relive some of the most horrifying events in my life. Time did not and could not heal those wounds- **only** JESUS could do that! Unforgiveness gave root to bitterness and bitterness gave root to anger; anger gave root to witchcraft which I used to control others so no one would ever control me again- I justified it as "healthy manipulation", Witchcraft gave root to rage and hidden behind my rage was fear.

There are a few moments in those hours I will never forget, God willing, as long as I live. If there was any doubt, about what Christ was doing for me, through these people, that doubt quickly fled, as Jeff and Jane called out a few specific demons. When "bitterness" came out of me there was such a foul taste in my mouth. It was the most bitter and disgusting thing I had ever tasted in my life. As soon as the demon left so did the taste. "Witchcraft" leaving was terrifying for me because it began speaking through me. I spoke in a deep and gruff voice in a language I did not know. Jeff told the demon to stop speaking in JESUS name and it listened to him for it is written, "...even the demons are subject to us through Your Name"

(Luke 10:17 LITV). As soon as "witchcraft" left, the demonic in me tried to attack Jeff. I was on the ground on all fours vomiting and spitting, when this happened. Jeff raised his hand and then placed it on my head and commanded the demon of rage to be loosed, in JESUS name, for whatever you bind on the earth will be, having been bound in Heaven. And whatever you loose on the earth will be, having been loosed in Heaven (Mark 18:18 LITV). I then instantly began to tremble and cowered in a corner in fear. Jeff then commanded the spirit of fear to leave me in JESUS name. Just when I thought it was over Jeff asked, "What is your name?" I in turn thought this was a retarded question, I was sure he knew my name. When I opened my mouth to say my name, the words, "Legion for we are many" proceeded instead. I was horrified! As soon as the legion left me, I jumped to my feet screaming with joy, "I am free!" I jumped on my husband proclaiming, "I am free!!!! I AM FREE!!!!" I felt so light as if a thousand pounds had been taken off of me. I thought for sure if someone didn't hold on to me I was going to float right out of there. Jeff and Jane were asking the Holy Spirit to fill in all of those spaces the demonic had resided in, for it is written, "Or do you not know that your body is a temple of the Holy Spirit in you, whom you have of God? And you are not your own, for you are bought with a price" 1 Corinthians 6:19. and "When an evil spirit comes out of a man, it goes through arid places seeking rest and does not find it. Then it says, 'I will return to the house I left.' When it arrives, it finds the house unoccupied, swept clean and put in order. Then it goes and takes with it seven other spirits more wicked than itself, and they go in and live there. And the final condition of that man is worse than the first." Matthew 12:43-45. For the first time in about twenty-five years, I could see Jesus again as I did as a tiny child. The "pillows" separating Jesus and me from that dreadful night all those years ago had finally fallen to the floor and I could run into the arms of my king once more! I told everyone in the room that I could see myself running into Jesus' arms. Surprisingly, I looked just like I did when I was a little girl. Jesus picked me up and twirled me around. I was free and it was all because of Him!

I never knew I was in bondage not to mention I wasn't even sure if I believed demons really existed. I knew nothing about deliverance ministry nor had any teachings whatsoever about what had just happened. NEVER. But I can tell you one thing…I knew FREEDOM in Christ as soon as I had it. When the demonic were gone, I knew they had been there and weren't now. I knew I was a new being. Jesus had set me free and now I knew Christ was not only real, but alive and well! I may not have known I was carrying demonic chains, but I sure knew when Jesus had taken them off.

I am grateful and often praise God for allowing me to experience my deliverance. Most people, I would venture to say, who are delivered from demons in Jesus' name are either completely unaware this has occurred or believe they just feel better because God answered their prayer. Because of the changes in my thinking, life and actions; I am utterly convinced of what Jesus did for me. I am thankful Jesus said follow the fruit because a good tree can not bear bad fruit nor can a bad tree bear good fruit (Matthew 7:17-18). My fruit is now good and satan cannot take that from me, not ever, God willing.

At this point I thought it was all over and life would go on as usual. I was very wrong about that. Jesus had only just begun a work in me and was nowhere near completing even this piece of it. The speakers had warned me I was now going to be aware of the battle over my mind and soul. They encouraged me to rebuke satan whenever he tried to come against what Jesus was doing in my life. They strongly advised me to always do so in the name of Jesus. I took everything they said very seriously and heeded their warning.

An hour or so later I was walking outside with my son wrapped in my arms. Excitement vibrated through my very being. My child looked at me right in my eyes and with bone chilling assertion plainly stated, "You know those prayers didn't work don't you?" I looked right passed my son and directly at the devil which was speaking through him and firmly rebuked it in JESUS name. The whole time it felt like there was still something in my throat. As soon as I rebuked the devil I spit another huge ball of phlegm out of my throat. I reasoned the devil had to have spoken through my son because there was no way my son, at four years old, had any idea of what had just taken place. My son then gave me a hug and tightly hung onto my neck.

That night, August 10, 2007, Jeff and Jane asked if anyone wanted to quickly testify. I was completely and totally on fire. I felt so free and so bold I could hardly contain myself. My hand shot up right away. I shared how I was free and was no longer afraid. I wanted everyone to have what I had. That was the first time I spoke in front of a crowd without fear. Just standing up there was victorious for me. I was definitely one of those people who had a fear of crowds and public speaking, but not anymore. Jesus was all I wanted to focus on. There was something else I noticed that night at service. I no longer struggled to understand Jeff and Jane, my stomach was not sore and I no longer looked like I was about to give birth. Jesus had delivered me.

The next night was Saturday and Jane was speaking again. As she began preaching, I noticed I started feeling like I was going to throw up again. I went outside to try and get some fresh air. I could still clearly hear everything she was talking about. Jane was preaching about repentance for not only my sins, but for sins of iniquity or sins of our family members that have been passed on through the generations. An example of this is alcoholism, rage or divorce. I immediately started repenting for every sin that ran in my family and asked God to forgive my family for sinning against Him. I cried out to God and asked him to reveal to me the sins of iniquity in me; I wanted nothing but Him in me. So God began searching me. As He revealed the iniquity I repented, sought forgiveness and asked Jesus to break the iniquity off of my children as well. I knew if this stuff, these curses, these sins, had been passed down to me, then I had probably passed it on to my children.

On my knees I cried out to God as I looked towards heaven. The brilliance of the starry sky had me in complete awe of God's creation. I knew God could hear my plea and He would answer me. This overwhelming power came over me as I was repenting. It was as if I could see, but not necessarily with my eyes, the Holy Spirit coming towards me. I was immediately face-down in the dirt. My body felt so heavy. I tried to lift my pinky finger, but to no avail. The weight that had come over my body was intense. For the first time in my adult life, I could feel the presence of the Living God. I was in this state for what seemed to be quite awhile. He didn't say anything to me. He just let me soak in His presence under the weight of His glory.

Jeff and Jane left the next day, but before they left they prophesied (gave a message from God) to our family. Part of the prophecy which was really exciting for me was God had told them He was going to give me a new name no one in my family had ever had. I instantly became very excited knowing what the name was. My name is Rauel Malachi (friend of God/ God's messenger).

> **He who has an ear, let him hear what the Spirit says to the churches. To him who overcomes I will give to eat of the hidden manna, and will give to him a white stone, and in the stone a new name written, which no man knows except he who receives it . (Rev 2:17)**

Our family was invited to stay for the next week of camp as volunteers, baking and cleaning. We gratefully accepted the offer to stay. God completely rearranged my brain that week. It felt as if I was a two year old child learning everything new for the first time. Everything was different now and so was I. I needed to relearn and unlearn almost everything I had ever known about Jesus and the realities of life. God began teaching me about all things through the Holy Spirit (John 14:26).

> **Do not conform any longer to the pattern of this world, but be transformed by the renewing of your mind. Then you will be able to test and approve what God's will is-His good, pleasing and perfect will.**
> Romans 12:2 NIV

I spent most of the week on my knees with my head on the ground completely humbled before God on His throne. I will never be able to fully express the gratitude and love I now had for Jesus and what He had done for me.

At the closing of the week my husband and I were invited to be the recreational directors and bakers for youth week. It still amazes me how God used us immediately after transforming me only a few days prior. I was delighted we were asked to stay and help out because I really didn't want to leave camp at all. I was not ready to be back in the world. The desire to know God more, to understand why Jesus would die for me, and how the Holy Spirit was somehow deeply involved consumed my every waking thought.

Youth week was an amazing week. We witnessed huge acts of God in the youth. One night as almost all of the youth were praying I was at a loss for words and yet wanted to still be able to pray, but didn't know what to say. In my struggling efforts, all of a sudden I started praying in a language unknown to me. I had been blessed with the gift of tongues. I looked behind me to discover Calum, one of the youth, was praying over me asking God to give me the gift of tongues. Praise be to God!

Camp was now over and it was time to return home. Our family had become very attached to a couple of the youth over the summer. I was grieved not only believing we may never see them again, but I was also concerned about what would become of them once they returned home.

Even though the tears would not stop rolling down my checks, I knew God had everything under control and Jesus would be there to see us all through it. It was time to go home and face the world. Jesus had saved me and I wanted the world to know of His love, grace and mercy.

And you, who were once alienated and enemies in your mind by wicked works, yet now He has reconciled in the body of His flesh through death, to present you holy and without blemish, and without charge in His sight, if indeed you continue in the faith grounded and settled, and are not moved away from the hope of the gospel, which you have heard and which was proclaimed in all the creation under Heaven
~Colossians 1:21-23~ MKJV

Standing on the Word

O taste and see that the LORD is good: blessed is the man that trusteth in him. Psalm 34:8 KJV

Once we were home, there was a realization there was a lot of physical work to do in the house. Our family went through everything we owned. Our oldest daughter willingly removed approximately fourteen big black garbage bags from her room alone. By the time we were finished going through the clothing, I had about two pairs of pants and three shirts left. All of my other clothing was too small, revealing or sensual. We took out five laundry hampers of books that all had something about witchcraft (witches, ghosts, goblins, dragons, wizards, magic, etc). As a family, we sorted through our movies as well. Almost every movie we owned brought disgrace to God and we didn't even realize it. The children were active participants in going through our belongings. We prayed and asked God to show us what needed to go and what could stay. The movies were what really surprised me because I thought I was always so careful about what the kids watched. It was horrifying when the Holy Spirit revealed to us how much sinful content was in our movies. Again there was a lot of witchcraft in what we were watching, and as for Marc and I, there was a lot of sexual immorality, violence and foul language. The last big thing for us was going through our music. I always really liked music and now I wasn't so sure about what we were listening to and what we were exposing our children to. I wanted nothing to do with what the world had to offer any more because the cares of this world, and the deceit of riches, and the lust about other things entering in, choke the Word, and it becomes unfruitful (Mark 4:19 MKJV). I knew what embracing the world and its beliefs and values had done to my life and now that I had freedom, because of Jesus, the lusts of the world had no pull on me anymore.

Grace and peace be multiplied to you through the knowledge of God and of Jesus our Lord, according as His divine power has given to us all things that pertain to life and godliness, through the knowledge of Him who has called us to glory and virtue, through which He has given to us exceedingly great and precious promises, so that by these you might be partakers of the divine nature, having escaped the corruption that is in the world through lust. 2 Peter 1:2-4

With everything we had taken out of the house, some of it went straight into the garbage, some we sold in a garage sale and the rest we gave away. Not everything we had was evil or wicked, but we coveted and turned our materialistic items into idols and so they had to go. Our house was starting to feel like a safe place to be and I was very grateful to God for sending the Holy Spirit to teach us what was good and what wasn't.

Not too long after being home, I felt like I needed to apologize to a few people and to submit myself to the authorities in our church. The Holy Spirit showed me how I was using the spirit of Jezebel, which is the demonic that had the characteristics of Jezebel from the bible, to manipulate and control others. I repented but God told me I needed to confess my sins to a group of people from our church, for it is written, "Therefore, make it your habit to confess your sins to one another and to pray for one another, so that you may be healed. The prayer of a righteous person is powerful and effective" (James 5:16). I asked God to show me who He wanted present and when He did I was a bit fearful. The group comprised of eight people including my husband. I had to admit and seek forgiveness for manipulating men with my body, and for trying to control the leaders in my church or conversations held by the leaders. I had to confess always trying to seek the attention of others and apologize for undermining the authority of our pastor and our elders by showing little to no respect for the position God had put them in. The weight of humility was heavy yet freeing. The Lord told me to confessed how I was disrespectful to my husband and his authority in our home including how I always wanted to be the head of house even though God said it is to be Christ, then my husband, and then me (1 Corinthians 11:3). The experience was very humbling. Everyone sat quietly as I spoke and asked a few questions to clarify what I was confessing. The group then prayed for my husband and me.

God continued to clean up my life through His spoken and written word, dreams and visions. God had given me a scripture in a dream one night. I was told I was still grieving Jesus. Devastated, I asked how this could be. So many things had changed in my life. How could this be? It was incredibly heartbreaking. I wanted to know what God wanted me to do. This is the scripture I received…

> **I am afraid that when I come my God may again humble me before you and that I may have to grieve over many who formerly lived in sin and have not repented of their impurity, sexual immorality, and promiscuity that they once practiced.** 2 Corinthians 12: 21 ISV

I knew almost immediately what I needed to repented of. The Holy Spirit had been teaching me about soul ties (1 Samuel 18:1) which to be put simply, is one person's connection to another person.

My next question for God was how these soul ties were formed. The Holy Spirit taught me some are made from conception (both God given and in iniquity) such as with parents, through cutting a covenant (sexual relationships), dating and friendships. God then went a little deeper. He was teaching me about how it was a sin to have sex with anyone who I was not married to, and I should have remained a virgin until I was married to my husband. Also, I should not have even lived with my husband until we were married. All of this was very sinful and grieved Him tremendously.

> **Let marriage be kept honorable in every way, and the marriage bed undefiled. For God will judge those who**

commit sexual sins, especially those who commit adultery. Hebrews 13:4 ISV

The Holy Spirit has also taught me about dating. After reading the bible from cover to cover I discovered something very interesting. There was no dating. I did not find one single case. No one ever dated one person and then decided they weren't "the one" and then dated someone else until they found the "right one". Parents did not encourage this either. In discovering this truth, God lead me to the conclusion that since we know satan mimics what God has designed, dating is the mimic for marriage. I firmly believe God created marriage. I also believe satan manipulated it into what we now call dating. Jesus also stated, "Anyone who stares at a woman with lust for her has already committed adultery with her in his heart" (Matthew 5:28). I don't know about you, but every time I "liked" a guy lust was always involved. I always thought about how good looking he was or how I wanted to be "intimate" with him. This was lustfulness.

There were also soul ties with friends. Some were put in place by God and others were not for it is written; "do not be mislead: 'Bad company corrupts good character.' Come back to your senses as you ought, and stop sinning; for there are some of you who are ignorant of God- I say this to your shame" (1 Corinthians 15:33-34). I was definitely ignorant.

With all of this new knowledge I took a look at the scripture again…

lest in my coming again my God will humble me with you; and I shall mourn many who have already sinned, and not repenting over the uncleanness, and fornication, and lustfulness which they have practiced. 2 Corinthians 12: 21 ISV

I sat in the washroom and began repenting for these past sins. As I sat there the faces of people in my past began to surface. God taught me to pray like this when repenting and breaking off my ungodly soul ties:

Father God, please forgive me for my ungodly soul tie that I formed with _____. Jesus thank you breaking the tie at the foot off the cross rendering it powerless and for the revelation of my freedom from it. In Jesus' mighty name. Amen.

After a long time of praying and repenting, I felt like yet another weight had been lifted off of my shoulders. My relationship with my husband began to change immediately. I worked up the courage and told my husband about what God had taught me and in his own time, he too broke off his soul ties. The thoughts and dreams of Daniel came to a stop and I no longer longed for him. I also broke the vow of everlasting love through the power of Christ and repented for making it in the first place. I was now free to give that piece of myself to my husband. My marriage was continuing to be transformed by God.

Praise you Jesus for the finished work of the cross and complete freedom from sin. That you died once and for all that sin would never reign in me again. It is gone dead and buried.

*One thing I have desired from
Jehovah, that I will seek after: that I
may dwell in the house of Jehovah all
the days of my life, to behold the
beauty of Jehovah, and to
pray in His temple.
~Psalm 27:4~ MKJV*

Love Covers

Above all, love each other deeply, because love covers over a multitude of sins. 1 Peter 4:8 (NIV)

Rural Manitoba winter had set in and so did my first trial...

The trial of your faith (being much more precious than that of gold that perishes, but being proven through fire) might be found to praise and honor and glory at the revelation of Jesus Christ 1 Peter1:7 MKJV

In the middle of November I received a devastating phone call from my little brother Jonathan. My brother had gotten married in June and his new bride had just been diagnosed with breast cancer. My heart started breaking into a million pieces as I heard the pain in his voice. He kept saying at twenty-six years old, he was too young to be a widower. I tried to comfort him but it was to no avail. I told him if he needed anything no matter what, he could call me day or night. He asked me to pray for him and so I prayed for him over the phone for the first time in our lives. After hanging up the phone, I wept. Oh, how I just wanted to tuck into my husband's arms.

Calum came over for the weekend and that Saturday night, while we were searching for movies online, I noticed something in my husbands search bar. The word sex popped up when he had pressed the letter s. I wasn't sure if Calum had noticed or if my husband had noticed either, but I had. Something wasn't right and I became very restless. After everyone had gone to bed, I took my husband's computer and started searching his history and temp files. To my complete horror, I discovered my husband had been looking at porn again. This was blow number two in seventy-two hours and I didn't know what to do. Before Jesus delivered me, I would get mad, and then go and drink and smoke. That was all given up when Jesus set me free and so I wasn't sure what to do with my emotions. In the middle of the night, I went outside and took a massive hissy fit. Crying out to God, I asked Him why and how this could be. I became very demanding of Him and then in my anger, I took a two by four and swung it at our well breaking it in half. Through my tear stained face, I started praying in tongues while pacing back and forth in the yard.

Finally, I went inside and woke Marc up. I demanded to know how long so I knew how and what to pray. In the middle of confronting Marc, I told him I was sick of the devil getting to him and I had intended to put an end to it. Marc, who had just been awoken from a dead sleep, denied it at first and then fessed up a few minutes later. I was angry, hurt, confused and distraught. How could this happen after everything Jesus had done for us this summer. How could I still be so easily deceived? I was sick and tired of the enemy having his way in my house and especially with my husband.

I cried out to Jesus for help. I was completely and totally broken. My heart was already aching enough learning two days prior my brother's wife had cancer, but to then learn my marriage was on the brink of no return, I wasn't sure if I was strong enough to handle this. I wanted to lean on my husband for , but now I had no one to turn to except Christ.

I can do all things through Christ who strengthens me. Philippians 4:13 MKJV

The next morning was Sunday and we headed off to church. Picking up a banner (flag) in church, I was committed to taking a stand against the devil's schemes (Ephesians 6:11 NIV). I was full of righteous anger against the wiles of the enemy and I wanted victory in Christ for all of those who were being oppressed or attacked by the devil. Something seemed different about that service; for the first time I raised my banner without fear of man or of condemnation. Nothing was going to stand between my love for God and me.

Lift up a banner in the land (Jeremiah 51:27). **You have given a banner to those who fear You, to lift it up because of the truth** (Psalm 60:4).

I didn't care what anyone thought about my love for my Savior or my desire to worship Him with everything I had in me. I was tired of the enemy getting all of the attention and God seemingly taking a back burner. Christ was in me and I was going to let my light shine that day. Satan did everything he could to get me to stop waving my banner. The Holy Spirit reminded me that my battle was not against flesh and blood but against the rulers, against the authorities, against the powers of this dark world and against the spiritual forces of evil in the heavenly realms (Ephesians 6:12 NIV). Instead of feeling anger towards those who were offended I was raising my banner, I felt pity. I knew they did not understand my whole world was crumbling around me and the only thing I had to hold onto was Jesus Christ, my Lord and Savior, the one who redeemed me and pulled me up from the fiery pit I had been living in. The only thing I could do in that very moment was to call on God, my refuge and strength, an ever-present help in trouble. (Psalm 46:1). Jesus has taught me I am to bless and not curse those who persecute me and so that is what I was determined to do (Romans 12:14, Matthew 5:44, Luke 6:28). It is no longer hard not sin in my anger or to seek revenge, because I remember revenge is God's job not mine (Romans 12:19). Mine is to love.

After returning home from church, I went straight to my room. I grabbed my bible and turned on worship music. There were a couple of songs in particular I played over and over. One of the songs I really held onto was called, *There Must Be a God* which talked about the wonders of God and how He is there for the prodigal sons. The song also spoke about how it is a long road we are traveling on to get home and we don't know how far we have left to go. Because we don't know how far we have left to go we can cry out for God's mercy asking Him not to forget us. I meditated on God's word all day and night. I did not leave my room or have anything to eat or drink.

I woke up the next morning with still no desire to leave my room. I had a CD player, some worship music and my bible. I had no intentions of going anywhere. I prayed, read my bible, worshiped and slept on and off all day and night. Again I had no food or drink. I spent the next day the same as the last two. No food or drink touched my lips for three days.

At around two in the morning on the third night, I was lying in my bed and I began to have a vision of our church. In the vision, I stood up and began testifying about what God's heart was for our church as a whole and for each of us as individuals. God had a cry of purity for His people. God was very specific about how sexual sin was oppressing our congregation. God was grieved over the use of pornography as well as the adulteries that were not only flamboyantly done, but the secret adulteries in the hearts of the people as well. God wanted to sanctify us and remove every form of wickedness from our lives, leaving nothing behind. We were being called to no longer live as hypocrites, but as those who were robed with righteousness. God wanted our congregation to know He loves them and how He wants them free from oppression. We were called to be holy and separate unto God, but we were not walking in righteousness. We had given up our first love which was Jesus. As I stood testifying, God had me ask the warriors if they would be willing to take a stand with me through Jesus to put an end to the oppression in our church; if they would be willing to set the captives free. The warriors in our church started to stand up. We had our spiritual armor on. Each one who stood, stood firm and with great boldness. There was no question they were anointed by God to go forward into battle. God then revealed to me that not all of His chosen would stand because of fear and unbelief. Those who stood then walked to the front of the church and invited people to come forward for prayer. A man stood up in the back of the church and came forward. He got on his knees and started repenting. This man was one of the last people anyone would have thought to not only to come forward, but to be the first in line. After seeing this, people in the congregation started coming forward to repent and humble themselves before God and man (James 4:7&10, Romans 12:10).

I was so pumped up I went to the computer and started typing out the vision in an e-mail to one of my closest friends. The next thing I knew, it was around four in the morning and I had written ten different letters to twelve people about the vision. Each letter began the same, but then had varying differences in the middle and an ending that was unique to each person. I wrote things about the people I had no way of knowing. Sitting back in my chair a twinge of fear crept over me. What had just happened? Where did I get the information from? Was it even true? What if it was? What if it wasn't? I wondered what I was going to do with these letters I called words of encouragement, so I asked God what to do with them. He told me to give four of the letters out immediately, but the other six needed to be given under the authority of first my husband, and then the pastor. I asked my husband first and he gave me permission. Then I waited a few days continuing to pray about the last six.

After resting under the wings of God for three days with no food or drink, I felt a peace over me I cannot begin to properly explain. I was in total awe of God. I knew God had everything under control and we were going to be okay as a family, but there was still a long road yet to travel. I was in total awe of God.

Finally, I wrote an e-mail to my pastor along with the letters. I confessed in my e-mail that I was writing from a place of complete brokenness. God had been so good to me in these last few months, but particularly in these last weeks. My entire world had been rocked and I am so thankful that God was here with me to hold me up. I wrote that I could honestly say that if God didn't show me such grace and mercy this summer, I didn't think I would have been able to endure these struggles I was facing. After explaining my mental and spiritual condition, I poured out my testimony from childhood to my deliverance. It was important to me that my pastor knew how desperately I wanted to continue in grace and obedience in accordance with God's plans for my life. Also, to share with him how God taught me that there are authorities who have been placed above me and my pastor was one of these authorities. Submitting to not only my husband, but my pastor as well, used to be a huge challenge for me. Typically I would rebel against authority or at the very least manipulate it to serve me. Praise God He can change even a sinner like I was!

After writing the e-mail, I just sat there with my hands on my head staring at the screen. I took a deep breath in filing my cheeks and then slowly let the air out of my lungs. That was one of the hardest e-mails I had ever written. Trembling, I placed the e-mail in my saved folder. My nerves almost made me sick to my stomach. This was such a crossroads in my life and the only thing I knew to do was to trust God. Jesus being my rock in that moment was key to my survival. Without the love of Christ, I would be totally lost. Over a week had past before I worked up the courage to send the letter to my pastor. Once the send button was pressed, there was no turning back. In my mind, I was taking a chance on God and as always, God was faithful.

My pastor reviewed the letters I called words of encouragement and asked me to remove some parts, which I immediately did. God had told me to walk in submission and I had no intentions of doing anything to the contrary. Even though I had permission from my church, I was still not ready to give out the letters that were now being called prophesies. When it came down to it, the bottom line had my name attached to it and I wanted to be doubly sure I had truly received the letters from God the Father and not my own delusions, or worse from satan.

Within days of all of this occurring, I received a call from my brother with the news his wife's condition was rapidly deteriorating. They had learned she had stage four breast cancer and there was little hope she would live. Jonathon asked me to come to the city to help him at home. Without hesitation, I hopped on the bus first thing the next morning.

Hoping to know the final outcome of the situation, I asked God if she was going to live. God had reminded me He saved people in three ways- from the fire, through the fire and by the fire. From the fire means you never experience the crisis or problem. Through the fire means God walks you through the fire and you become stronger and in the end it may look like you lost something, but you have not truly lost anything only gained (Job is a good example of this or the 3 in the furnace). By the fire means you must experience the full suffering and that this is the end of the line such as death, losing out on something God had planned for you. God does not allow bad things to happen because He is mean, unkind or unloving, but rather bad things happen as a result of sin in a fallen world. Some people only turn to Him for salvation when life has hit a huge crisis. God loves us enough to allow the crisis so that we may obtain salvation through His Son Jesus Christ. God placed in my heart the reality that she would only be saved by the fire. I knew then she was going to die. Immediately, I began praying for her salvation. There was a group of people in our church who began praying for her on a continual basis as well.

My oldest daughter and I arrived in Winnipeg where my brother was waiting for our arrival. The cold winter's air blew right through us. As I gave him a big hug, I could feel his heart breaking in my arms. Through the sounds of the busy city there was silence in our hug, as if the whole world had frozen in that moment. There was so much fear and pain in my little brother's heart and there was nothing I could do to stop it from shattering. It was such a blessing God had reconciled Jonathon and me only a year prior, after years of no contact with each other.

Schooling for my oldest became second priority as she helped me take care of our family. We made meals, did the house cleaning and prayed continually. My brother's wife had a daughter who was a year and a half older than my daughter. She was scared and hurting. She did not even really know who we were, and yet had been thrown into our lives due to this tragic unfolding in her life. Not only did she not know us, but what little she had heard was not good. Her mother did not like me at all. Oddly enough though, I couldn't help but feel love and compassion for these two females in my brother's life. Jesus had placed a supernatural love for them in my heart. I believe this to be true because I loved them as if I had always known them and cared for them.

A week later, Marc came to pick us up. I needed to go home for a couple of days to spend time with our four year old and six year old who were in between babysitters for the first time in their lives. Before returning home, Mark and I got into a huge fight in my brother's kitchen. I had not been in a huge fight with my husband since my deliverance back in August. The words flying out of my mouth were cruel and I soon became out of control. Out of no where and uncontrollably, I threw something at my husband that just missed his head. We then headed into the bedroom to fight some more. Shortly there after, I realized what was happening…I had given a foothold to the devil. Quickly I pleaded with my husband to pray over me. Our fighting stopped instantly and my husband began praying over me. I apologized, asking for his forgiveness. I sought forgiveness of my heavenly Father and from Jesus who had set me free. It was completely devastating that this Rage had somehow taken control of me again, and I had not even realized it. How could I have been so foolish? I asked God how this happened and He told me it was because I had not truly forgiven my husband for looking at pornography the month before. I knew God's words were true. Even though I had gone to war for my husband, I had not forgiven him for his transgression. Forgiving Marc was too hard on my own; I needed Jesus to help me. Broken and hurt, I asked Jesus to help me forgive my husband completely because I could not do it in my own strength. Mentally I knew forgiving did not mean I was saying what he did was okay, but my heart struggled with the pain of the adultery. After choosing to forgive my husband, I felt much better and at greater peace almost seconds after.

Over the next month, I was back and forth between home and my brother's. On one of the trips home, a group of our friend's, Marc, and I got together to pray for my brother's wife. As we were praying I had a vision of Jesus sitting on her bed with His hand raised outward. It was as if He had created a force field around Himself and my brother's wife. As Jesus was sitting on her bed, completely at peace as a demon tried to enter into His force field. The enemy could not infiltrate the premises at all. Looking at an angel, Jesus shook His head as if to say, "Can you believe this guy?" With much relief, I shared the vision with the group. One of our friends then shared he had seen Jesus in her hospital room holding her hand. To me this was affirmation of what I had seen. I did not know what any of this meant, but I believed we had been given evidence of a break through.

As soon as I got home, I called my brother and told him about the visions. I think he thought I was a bit out of my mind, but I believed I needed to tell him. He had been saying since I had come back from camp I was on blue Kool-Aid (in other words- slang for crazy). Even though my brother thought I was crazy, he hesitantly decided to tell his wife what had happened in our prayer group. She unexpectedly told my brother she didn't think it was that crazy. She went on to tell him she had accepted Jesus as her Lord and Savior that day. She then explained how as she was accepting Jesus, she felt as if He was sitting beside her holding her hand. To me this was one of the most exciting moments I had experienced in Christ since He saved me. I knew she was going to die here in body, but was going on to live forever with Jesus.

Christmas day was spent with Marc and the children at my brother's. My brother spent those few days up at the hospital with his wife and her child. This Christmas there was no tree, no gifts, no turkey on the table, or extended family to celebrate the birth of the Messiah. Yet this, however, was the best Christmas we had ever spent together as a family. We spent the day playing with our children giving thanks to God for sending us His son. I think we ate hot dogs for super accompanied with thanksgiving and laughter. It was the first Christmas I had ever spent stress free. I was in such admiration of my children who not once complained they had no gifts to open or tree to gaze at or big meal to eat. They just spent the day joyously spending time with their family. Their sacrifice was so selfless and a shining example of Christ.

My thoughts often drifted to my brother and his family that day as they were spending their last Christmas together in a small hospital room. They too only had each other and it wasn't for much longer. My brother's wife had lost her vision the week before, and so she couldn't even see her daughter's face or look into her eyes that Christmas. She couldn't see the love in my brother's eyes or the lights on the Christmas tree. This was the first year I truly appreciated what Christ had done for us by coming to planet earth to humbly be born as a baby out of the womb of a young woman. That Christmas, God blessed me with the ability to see past the glitz and glam of what we now call Christmas. I was convicted with the reality I had never truly celebrated Christmas before. My heart had always been ungrateful and selfish when it came to Christmas and not really focused on what Christ had done to cause the whole world to celebrate that day. God used this woman who had never liked me before to teach me about His Son.

Some people pitied my brother's family questioning why God would allow this to happen especially at this time of the year. I gently explained how God chose the perfect time if this were to happen anyway. He graciously chose the one time of the year where it is impossible to forget He was here and not only proved His existence to mankind, but came to die so people like me and my sister in-law could live. My brother and I were grateful God would honor us at this time with the evidence of His existence all around us. What a mighty God we serve.

Time was rapidly speeding ahead drawing close to the end of my sister-in-law's life. In the last week of her life, one of our friends willingly drove over two hours to pray and to share the gift of communion with her. In this tiny little hospital room, we gathered around my sister-in-law to remember the sacrifice Jesus had made for us two-thousand years ago. God taught me a couple of valuable lessons that night. The first was how to be a faithful and willing servant. I was overwhelmed with such gratitude because this friend was willing to leave his wife and children on that cold winter's night to drive hours away for a woman he did not know. Secondly, I did not realize you could have communion outside of a church building. I had always believed only a pastor could do that. God taught me about the scriptures explaining the true purpose of communion which was the remembrance of Christ's sacrifice. I always knew why we had communion, but I never grasped it in my heart or realized how sacred this act was. Our friend was there for only a few short minutes and then returned on his long journey home.

There was such a peace in the room that night and I was thankful to have been apart of this piece of her life. Over the course of a few weeks, she went from wanting nothing to do with me to having me spend the last three days of her life with her. My heart still weeps over this moment in time. I am not sure I will ever fully understand why God honored me of all people to hold the hand of this woman while her life slipped away.

> **You have heard that it was said, "You shall love your neighbor" and hate your enemy;** (*Lev. 19:18*) **but I say to you, Love your enemies; bless those cursing you, do well to those hating you; and pray for those abusing and persecuting you, so that you may become sons of your Father in Heaven.** Matthew 5:43-45 LITV

I spent those three days brushing the rotting flesh from her teeth, feeding her, and bathrooming her, but more importantly holding her hand, rubbing her head and reading God's word to her. God allowed me to read Matthew through to Titus before she passed away.

The night before she died I had an overwhelming urge to send my children home. God provided a way when it seemed there was going to be no way of getting them home. Only through God's grace did I learn a friend of mine was in the city visiting her son. She was more than willing to take my children back for me.

That night my brother stayed at the hospital with his wife and me. I curled my little brother into me as we slept together on a tiny hospital bed. It felt like it did when were little children scared in the middle of the night. I wished there was something I could do to ease Jonathon's pain. He seemed so strong and yet so helpless all at the same time. It took everything I had to be strong for him. My heart ached so deeply for the pair of them. They would never even have an anniversary together. I knew God was sovereign and just but that didn't stop my heart from aching. My brother curled into me and I tried to fall asleep, but kept waking from the sound of her struggling to breathe. One of the times I woke up I was selfishly irritated by the sound and had a hard time forgiving myself for that brief moment I lacked compassion for a woman who was in her last hour. After saying a prayer I fell back asleep. Around four a.m. I started weeping uncontrollably hard. My sobbing was so bad I had to leave the room to not wake my brother who was sleeping soundly. I cried out to God and pleaded for mercy for her life. I wanted her to live so very badly, for God to give her a second chance. I knew God ultimately knew what was best and He was a righteous and just God, but my heart was breaking for my little brother and his family. After a few minutes I was able to stop crying long enough to go back in the room. I went to the side of her bed and held her hand. She was so frail and you could see death all over her. I knew there wasn't much time left. I was hoping God was going to let me finish reading the New Testament to her before He took her, but that wasn't possible. Curling back into my brother I just gazed at his wife. Softly I whispered it was okay she could go now, I was there with my brother. Then I asked God to end her suffering. Humbly, I told God I wanted to be with my brother when it happened so Jonathon would not be alone.

Just after seven, suddenly both my brother and I woke up to check on his wife. She was still holding on so we decided to get a couple more minutes of sleep before we got up. We then woke around fifteen minutes later to the sounds of soft weeping and sniffling. The nurses were all standing beside her bed. She had silently passed away while we slept. I may never understand why we were not awake to hold her hand as she left us, but I believe Jesus was right there holding her tight.

Looking at my brother, we both broke down in tears. It was all over. The depth of his sorrow and the crumbling of his heart beneath his grief were felt by everyone in the silence of the room. I had come to love this woman who was no longer my enemy, and I too was going to miss her terribly.

We left the room and went out into the hall and cried. The staff slowly, one by one, approached us and gave us hugs filled with tears. There was so much pain on the ward it was almost too hard to stomach. Not only were the nurses crying, but the orderlies and the doctors were crying also. They confided in my brother they too had come to love her and were going to miss her.

As I sat at one end of the hall with my brother in my arms, I looked down to the nurses' station where the entire staff gathered in hugs and tears. Sitting in that long dark hallway I knew God had done such an amazing work on that ward and even if no one else knew what He had done, I knew and was eternally grateful.

The memorial was about a week later and then it was over. I continued to visit my brother on and off to help him with the housework and to be an emotional support for him and her daughter. I wished I could have done more for him, but I continued to pray for strength for their family and that God would bless them.

Remembering the last seventy-two hours of my sister-in-law's life, was constantly on the forefront of my thoughts. Somehow my human brain was trying to comprehend and make sense of God's ways. I knew my being there was planned by God, but I desperately wanted to know why. However, I have come to accept that I may never fully understand what God had done in that moment and I am okay with that. I do, however, know I will forever be blessed by learning you can come to love your enemy to the point they become a member in the body of Christ with you. This is one of God's most profound and greatest mysteries to me. Love truly covers over a multitude of sin and I am only beginning to barely scratch the surface of understanding what this means (Proverbs 10:12).

Then Peter came up and asked him, "Lord, how many times may my brother sin against me and I have to forgive him? Seven times?" Jesus said to him, "I tell you, not just seven times, but seventy-seven times!"
~Matthew 18:21-22~ ISV

Freedom in Christ

And the Lord is the Spirit; and where the Spirit of the Lord is, there is freedom. 2 Corinthians 3:17 LITV

During the first year of my freedom, The Holy Spirit had taught me (1 John 2:27, John 14:26) so many things about God the Father and Jesus the Son of the Living God. Jesus is the Way, the Truth and the Life and no one comes to the Father except through Him (John 14:6). I had fallen in love with my Redeemer. However, I was still angry at God for seemingly not protecting me from the abuse, or so I had thought.

At this point God had taught me humans have a free will and some of them choose to use that free will for complete and utter wickedness. I was given the ability to see what had happened spiritually with my biological father. This explained the why and how questions I had about the abuse, but there was still something paining me. I needed to know why Jesus would let this happen.

July 19, 2008, Jesus gave a revelation that I needed to believe I was totally free from my past. I sat in the Sheep Shed at camp while our guest speaker delivered an amazing message. He had informed us there were two angels in the room standing guard, but did not mention where. I was sure there was one only a few feet away from me. After the service I asked the speaker about the location of one of the angels and sure enough he affirmed there was an angel standing by me. The speaker told me to talk to Jesus and ask Him if I could approach the angel and then walk in obedience. He told me to start in the back corner of the room and slowly approach the area the angel was in, but not to move until God said it was okay to advance.

Right away I started talking to Jesus. He spoke to me as a friend or brother that night. He asked me if I loved Him; right away the scripture about Him asking Peter if he loved Him popped into my mind (John 21:15). I smiled and more than likely blushed a little replying, "You know that I love you." He then told me to take three steps forward. Jesus then asked me again, "Rauel, do you love me?" I could feel Him smiling as He asked. I smiled back and said, "Lord you know that I do." I then went to take a step, but He told me not to. Jesus then told me to take three more steps forward. Good thing I listened because if I hadn't I would have gotten hit by the door. He then asked me for a third time if I loved Him. Again I smiled and told Him He knew that I loved Him. Then things got serious. Jesus told me to begin worshipping Him and so I did. As I worshipped Him the sounds of the other people began to fade away. Being in His presence was amazing yet fearful all at the same time. He began to explain to me I had always believed He let satan molest me through my dad and He did not protect me from such evil. This was not the truth. Jesus asked me if I knew why I had huge memory gaps in my life I could never remember. He asked me not because He didn't know the answer, but because He wanted me to think about the question. I began to realize I really remembered very little of the abuse even though I knew it happened on a regular basis. Jesus then showed me how He protected my mind and sealed my spirit so that the demonic could not touch it. Man has free will and so chooses to do things that are outside the will of God, however, Jesus stopped satan from harming my spirit. Jesus then revealed to me the demonic had abused nothing more than a pile of dirt for it is written, for dust you are, and to dust you shall return (Genesis 3:19). Our flesh has memory in it and so my flesh needed to be healed because it could remember what happened, but my spirit (that which lives forever) was not harmed. Satan had control over me through a lie. The lie was that Jesus did not protect me. The truth was Jesus had protected the part of me that shall live forever. The will of man only harmed that which is dying from the moment it comes into existence. Tears started streaming down my face. Jesus allowed me to remember enough of the abuse to make sense of what was going on. If I remembered everything I more than likely would have lost my mind. Jesus never abandoned me. Jesus truly loved me and he had always been there protecting me right from the very beginning. There is much freedom in this truth. So what if satan had a field day with my skin? The sins of my flesh were no longer in control of me and therefore neither could satan control me. This Truth has completely set me free from my past. I thanked Jesus for this revelation. He in turn asked me to dance before Him to show His angel how much I loved Him and to show him what Jesus had done for me. With much joy and love I danced for my King, my Savior, my Redeemer, my Friend, Jesus Christ, Son of the Living God.

At the end of the week, my husband was baptized in the lake and there was a huge change in him afterwards. I knew with Christ, my husband was going to be able to fight any temptation thrown at him. I also believe Jesus had redeemed him. My husband talks about the sins of his past in a very different manner than he used to. When he speaks I have respect for him and I know he now knows truth about his sin. I am so blessed to now have a healthy respect of who God has made my husband to be. Now, I also trust God with my husband and no longer try to "fix" Marc. It took me a long time to realize God's will and way in my husband's life was better than mine. I cannot praise God enough for restoring our marriage. I have such a love for this man it is almost impossible to describe. I am very excited about what God has planned for us in the future and the direction our lives are taking. One thing I believe for certain is that Jesus will be the focal point of our lives. With all of this change that preceded my husband's baptism, I was getting excited because it was soon going to be my turn.

The day of my baptism rapidly encroached. I was sitting in the Sheep Shed about to write the date in my notebook, but I could not remember the date so I leaned over to ask Marc. When he told me it was August 10th I became incredibly excited. I knew I was getting baptized that day, but I did not realize what day of the month it was. God perfectly planned it so I would be baptized on my one year anniversary of freedom. I was so giddy and filled with love for Him. What a beautiful gift Jesus had given me.

My baptism was beautiful. I was surrounded by my family and friends. A friend of ours sang and played the guitar as I walked towards the water. He played the song that says though none may follow I'll follow Jesus, and there is no turning back. My husband and Jeff then walked me into the water and I was water baptized in the name of the Father, the Son, and the Holy Spirit. I was completely clean and was as new as the first day of my birth.

I was soon back in the world walking out my Christian life. I have learned if we do not have love for one another, our works are for nothing. It is by love and through love that God dwells in us and does great things. I want to encourage you to forgive and to not hold a grudge, for this brings spiritual death. Pray for your pastors and leaders on a regular basis. Please, for the sake of the kingdom, live lives worthy of Christ. Do not buy into the excuses that limit the perfection God had established in you through His Son Jesus Christ. Ask God to increase your desire for Him and ask Him to teach you all things that will bring Him blessings and glory. Doing the will of God always comes with both heavenly rewards and often persecution. Yet God has told us to find joy in persecution (Luke 6:22, 23). And we know that the joy of the LORD is our strength (Nehemiah 8:10). I am only just beginning to understand what this means. I am so very blessed for when I feel like giving up on God's works, God never gives up on me. God is bringing me into a new season and I am excited to walk it out. I humbly request you pray for me that Jesus will continue to guide me and protect me from the slings and arrows of satan and his messengers. Also I ask that you pray the body of Christ will walk in humility for much ground is won for Jesus there. It is a time for new beginnings, a time for moving in the will of God, a time for signs and wonders, a time to heal the sick, cleanse the lepers, raise the dead, and cast out demons (Matthew 10:8 MKJV). The Spirit of the Lord is on me; because of this He has anointed me to proclaim the Gospel to the poor. He has sent me to heal the brokenhearted, to proclaim deliverance to the captives, and new sight to the blind, to set at liberty those having been crushed, to proclaim the acceptable year of the Lord (Luke 4:18-19, Isaiah

61:1-2 MKJV). For I have received freely, freely I will give (Matthew 10:8 MKJV). Blessed be the name of the Father, Son and Holy Spirit. Jesus loves you as do I through Him who has set me free. Believe in Christ Jesus for you too can be set free and those who are set free are free indeed (John 8:36).

God Bless <><

Rauel Malachi

Love must be sincere. Hate what is evil; cling to what is good. Be devoted to one another in brotherly love. Honor one another above yourselves. Never be lacking in zeal, but keep your spiritual fervor, serving the Lord. Be joyful in hope, patient in affliction, faithful in prayer. Share with God's people who are in need. Practice hospitality.

Bless those who persecute you; bless and do not curse. Rejoice with those who rejoice; mourn with those who mourn. Live in harmony with one another. Do not be proud, but be willing to associate with people of lower position.

Do not repay evil for evil. Be careful to do what is right in the eyes of everybody. If it is possible, as far as it depends on you, live at peace with everyone. Do not take revenge, my friends, but leave room for God's wrath, for it is written: "It is Mine to avenge; I will repay," says the Lord.

On the contrary:
"If your enemy is hungry, feed him; if he is thirsty, give him something to drink. In doing this, you heap burning coals on his head."

Do not be overcome by evil, but overcome evil with good.

~Romans 12:9-21~ NIV

Made in the USA
Charleston, SC
06 February 2011